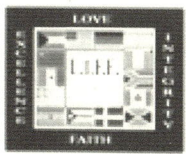  

Bishop Darryl F. Husband, Sr., D. Min.

©2008 Life More Abundant Ministries

Published by LuLu.com

Printed in the United States of America

©2008 Life More Abundant Ministries

Published by LuLu.com

All rights reserved. No part of this publication may be reproduced, stored in a retrieval system or transmitted in any form or by any means- electronic, mechanical, photocopy, recording or any other- without the prior written permission of the publisher. The only exception is brief quotations in printed reviews.

Unless otherwise noted; Scripture taken from the HOLY BIBLE, NEW INTERNATIONAL VERSION®. Copyright © 1973, 1978, 1984 International Bible Society. Used by permission of Zondervan. All rights reserved.

Scripture quotations identified as KJV are from the King James Version of the Bible.

Scripture quotations identified as AMP are taken from the Amplified® Bible, Copyright © 1954, 1958, 1962, 1964, 1965, 1987 by The Lockman Foundation Used by permission." (www.Lockman.org)

"Scripture taken from The Message. Copyright ©1993, 1994, 1995, 1996, 2000, 2001, 2002. Used by permission of NavPress Publishing Group."

Scripture taken from the NEW AMERICAN STANDARD BIBLE®, Copyright © 1960,1962,1963,1968,1971,1972,1973,1975,1977,1995 by The Lockman Foundation. Used by permission." (www.Lockman.org)

ISBN 978-0-557-00401-0

Dedication

To my wife, Sherrine,

I thank you for your love, understanding and prayers. You are truly so "Beautiful".

To my Children: Jason, who I owe and hope our years will soon find the time redeemed, Eric and Daytriel who are of my oldest ..., last but not least my awesome babies whom I cherish Darryl II, and Gabriella whom I pray will read this manuscript as you grow up, enter into his presence and become "Glory Carriers". It is your divine destiny.

To Bishop Wellington Boone and the F.O.I.C family, may we be walking Word, until the World is filled with the doctrine of Christ. Thanks for making me apart of a true family of ambassadors for the Kingdom.

Contents

DEDICATION..

ACKNOWLEDGEMENTS ....

INTRODUCTION 1

CHAPTER 1 *"THE 'ALTARED LIFE': MY PERSONAL PATH"* 2

CHAPTER 2 "THE POWER OF AN 'ALTARED' LIFE" 13

CHAPTER 3 "PREPARATION FOR THE JOURNEY" 26

CHAPTER 4 "THE TRAPS OF THE ENEMY" 36

CHAPTER 5 "THE RULES OF ENGAGEMENT" 46

CHAPTER 6 "THE TOOLS FOR ENGAGEMENT" 64

CHAPTER 7 "PRAYING THROUGH THE TEMPLE- THE OUTER COURT" 75

CHAPTER 8 "PRAYING THROUGH THE TEMPLE - THE INNER COURT" 99

CHAPTER 9 "THE INCENSE ALTAR: THE PLACE OF ILLUMINATION; THE HOLY OF HOLIES" 111

CHAPTER 10 "A CALL TO INTERCESSION" 122

REFERENCES 134

APPENDIX A 135

APPENDIX B 143

ABOUT THE AUTHOR 148

Acknowledgements

Several people have been instrumental in allowing this project to be completed. I would like to thank especially Joy M. Blathers, Jill Harris, Hugh Jones, Rev. Kevin James and Sharita Johnson for their hard work and dedication to this project. I would like to thank Pastor Dwayne Whitehead (my beloved Son in the Lord) and Dr. I.V. Hilliard, for their encouragement, advice and opportunities to minister at another level throughout the duration of this project. I would also like to thank Sandra A. Johnson, who worked on this manuscript tirelessly. I want to thank Mount Olivet Church, for your prayers, friendship and love while giving me patience to become a man of God. I love you and you can't do a thing about it!

Most of all, I give honor and praise to God, who called, anointed and equipped me to write this book. I glorify Jesus who redeemed me and set me free and the Holy Spirit for guiding me in all things.

Introduction

My Dear Friend,

    This is a letter and a guide to help you to enter into the presence of God by daily using simple, intentional tools and principles. How hungry are you for him? If it is your desire to know him intimately, to have a key to his residence, then I want to help you receive it.

    Prayer has such a bad stigma to it. It is time consuming. It takes knowledge to participate in it. What if I say the wrong thing? Is it not easier to allow my pastor to do it for me and let it be? Where do I start?

    I am convinced that the average Christian lives beneath their privileges because they have a distant, casual relationship with God. That relationship is managed by their pastor. Weekly, people stroll us into a large Christian day care center where we get to hear the voice of our Father and experience Him through the relationship and oversight of another. Often, we enjoy the time, but have no clue on how to get in touch with our Dad during the week, so that we can experience that same intimacy, instruction and empowerment.

    This guide will offer you several paths to the presence of God, from a biblical perspective. Everyday your relationship with Him will grow stronger; thereby you will grow into the image of God and become what I call, a "Carrier of the Glory". You cannot enter into His presence and not experience His awesome power, divine character, gifts and fruit. When you do that daily you will carry the "Glory of God" with you.

Chapter 1

"The 'Altared Life': My Personal Path"

It was 1996 and I was stuck in the rut of traditional religion and all of its secret ministerial bondages. I was tired of the old wine skins, but I kept pouring more wine into them (figuratively and literally). I knew that I wanted something more than the model I had seen, but honestly it was all I knew and fear of loneliness and ridicule hindered my pursuit. I decided however, to just explore some new venues to at least help the ministry the Lord had blessed me to Pastor. So I loaded up young leaders in the congregation and headed to a suburb of Chicago, Illinois called South Barrington, where we attended a Church Leadership Conference. The church was Willow Creek Community Church. The Pastor's name was Bill Hybels. This is where my journey began. It was there where I rekindled my passion for ministry and more importantly began a pursuit to dwell in the secret place of The Most High. Although the final result would take years, I understood in a small way why I was doing what I do (pastor). It was not the money, the fame, the titles or the freedom. It was because I really loved God. I just did not know how to truly be intimate with him. If the truth be told, I did not know anyone who had an intimate relationship with him. No one had ever taught me to go after Him with my words and my lifestyle.

Worship service was something people came to for a couple of hours and listened to music, a sermon, and some announcements and gave money. The church was a building that housed the worship event. Prayer was something we did with the

Pastor on Sunday and maybe over a meal. A Bible was a book we took to church on Sunday that the pastor preached from. God was someone we talked about as a distant overseer not a father who we are in relationship with or have unbroken fellowship.

My several trips to Willow began a spiritual awakening. I kept thinking, there is more to this than meets the eye. My journey needs to be extended beyond a week in the spring or fall of every year. Even though I sensed a tug to go deeper, to grow deeper, I always returned to the same friends, same church and same conversations. At least now I had seeds that were planted in me. The next several years would be a roller coaster ride that would eventually lead me to the throne room of God with a road map of how to return at will.

While Bill Hybels and the Willow team were the foundation for a brand new me, I feared the ridicule of my traditional peers. I secretly desired intimacy with God. For a few years they would see me in worship in the morning and then nursing a bottle of Cognac or wine while inhaling cigarettes at night. For years I fought my nightly fellowship with morning worship, so much so, that one of my colleagues called me "Doctor Jekyll and Mr. Hyde". He thought this was humorous, but I took it as a surgical knife that I would use to help me overcome.

I am not sure how I was initially introduced to Bishop Wellington Boone and Pastor Steve Parson, but they became my friends. I would golf with them when I could arise early enough to catch up with them. They were the first Pastors I knew that really were serious about the word of God and living holy. I am not saying I had not met anyone like this in all of my pastoring or ministry time. They talked about it with such passion outside of the walls of a church service and to my knowledge they were living the life they talked about. I never heard any talk otherwise about them. They were leaders of non-denominational churches, serious about God and I wanted to know what they had that I had not been exposed to. What was also great was that they played golf and were not "weird with their holiness". Wow! They spoke about ministry with such zeal that I was envious and wanted to know whether I had missed something. Who had reared them in this thinking? Where did they get their model from? When I talked to them about mentors or leaders they followed, I had never heard of the men in ministry they were speaking about. I was fully clothed in National Baptist Tradition.

However, there were two men in my convention, Pastor Ronald Bobo and now Bishop Michael Kelsey, who I loved and respected as righteous living brothers, but they were really outside of my close circle of friends (my hanging out buddies). One afternoon we were around the lobby talking and we agreed to do something very uncommon for me at a convention, go to one of our rooms and pray. I could not believe it. I was at a convention, in a room with some brothers in prayer. I felt strange at first because this was out of the norm. I had gone to rooms to drink and smoke. I had gone to rooms to meet women and "trash" talk with the guys (we called all of this fellowship), but never to pray. It was the first time I remember anyone ever even suggesting that we go somewhere and pray. Today would be different. We went to the room to pray and to encourage one another in the Lord. That day I made a decision that I was leaving the convention. I could not blame the convention, but I knew my life was not likely to change in that environment. I had invested too much time and energy in building the wrong kind of relationships. To make the kind of shift I knew I was destined to make was not going to be easy. I knew it would be next to impossible there. I did not know when or how I would do this. All I knew was that I could not keep enduring my present life as it was. I could not speak for the other two brothers, but our prayer time inspired me to take a leap of faith. I will be forever grateful to these men. They remain my friends today. We do not talk weekly, but we have traveled on mission trips together and I hold them as dear friends and partners in my spiritual development.

Out of the Country, But the Country Still In Me

Have you ever heard that saying? "You can take a man out of the country but you can't take the country out of the man". Well, I was away from the convention with all my worries gone. Right? Wrong! It's where I grew up. The lifestyle was bred in me. I was used to going to church. I was not used to being the church. I was accustomed to saying Jesus loves me, but I was not accustomed to saying I loved him, then living like it. I did believe however, that I needed to keep searching and help the members of my church to do the same. What a mess I thought. I have not a clue where to go or what to do and I am a pastor. How many other pastors are stuck in that condition as well? Who rescues those who are breaking and want to be broken, but do not know where to turn for fresh wind? My search was on to find some place where my people and I could find refuge. The worst part of the story is that the people didn't even know they were searching. They were satisfied in tradition. I think back now on what I call a rescue mission for us and I wonder as the captain of the ship was I wrong to carry them to waters they were unfamiliar with, even if I knew they were safer and better feeding grounds. The casualties seemed too much to bear even as I write this. What a painful sojourn. I thought *I* was stuck in something. I did not have a clue how deep my people were stuck. Church meetings and exoduses from our fellowship, as we moved towards seeking God, helped me understand clearly.

I took another group of young leaders (the first group was still around but, under attack), to Bethany World Prayer Center in Baker, Louisiana. Here we learned small groups (G-12) and an extension of what Willow Creek called "life in community", found in Acts 2. It was in Baker Louisiana that I began to hear about the urgency of prayer and prayer language. I still had a major problem praying and I was a Pastor. I did altar prayer on Sunday and prayed about my sermon. I prayed over my meals. I did not pray over my marriage, home or future. I did not have a format for prayer except the disciple's prayer which I now call the infant stage of prayer.

It was in Pastor Larry Stockstills' office where I was first introduced to the ministry of David Yonggi Cho, the Pastor of the world's largest church. He introduced me to a form of prayer that taught me how to pray for an hour or longer. He gave me a copy of Cho's version of the temple prayer. After I received that prayer, I spent many Sunday mornings at the altar using it. It was a painful time of weeping and washing away guilty stains. Slowly I learned to pray for an hour, but something was still missing. A part of that prayer was still foreign to me.

In All Thy Getting, Get Understanding

The next stop on my journey was a place called World Changers Church International. While I had heard of the baptism of the Holy Spirit way back in college and even spoke in tongues once, I was uncertain about it and feared doing it publically. I was also too "full of education" not to be able to explain why I was doing it. There was no preaching or teaching on this subject in my circle that made any sense. It was in the word, but I had never heard of a person in my church who exercised it. I do not ever remember hearing a sermon on it at the convention or in any church I grew up in, except my cousin's Pentecostal church which I visited once. They didn't really count though. Their services were three and four hours long and I convinced myself that nobody who really knew God acted like that. I thought they were way out there and I only went because I missed him when he left our home church. It was at a Creflo Dollar conference for leaders that I came face to face with understanding. I heard the following explanation and I knew I was released to speak and teach it to my church. Pastor Dollar said, "This prayer language is a language that neither can you understand, so you cannot mess it up, nor is it one the devil can understand, so he cannot mess it up". It was just enough for me to get going. I began to study the word of God. 1 Corinthians 14:2 and 4-5 says, *"For one who speaks in an [unknown] tongue speaks not to men but to God, for no one understands or catches his meaning, because in the [Holy] Spirit he utters secret truths and hidden things [not obvious to the understanding]... He who speaks in a [strange] tongue edifies and improves himself, but he who prophesies [interpreting the divine will and purpose and teaching with inspiration] edifies and improves the church and promotes growth [in Christian wisdom, piety, holiness, and happiness]... Now I wish that you might all speak in [unknown] tongues...* Then I read Jude 1:20, which says, *"But you, beloved, build yourselves up [founded] on your most holy faith [make progress, rise like an edifice higher and higher], praying in the Holy Spirit.* Next I read Romans 8:26, which says, *So too the [Holy] Spirit comes to our aid and bears us up in our weakness; for we do not know what prayer to offer nor how to offer it worthily as we ought, but the Spirit Himself goes to meet our supplication and pleads in our behalf with unspeakable yearnings and groaning too deep for utterance.* From these passages I began to build an understanding of why every Christian should be filled with the Holy Spirit and pray in tongues. Do we all need to encourage ourselves? Do we all need our faith to be built up? Do we all need help in our prayer life so that we pray the perfect will of God and see results? The answer to these questions is all the same, absolutely, unequivocally, yes.

Later in my search on the subject, I discovered a book by Mahesh Chavda called, The Hidden Power of Speaking In Tongues, in which he calls tongues, "the language of glory". In Chapter one of his book, I read the final point that helped my desire and freedom for praying in tongues. Chavada writes,

"Not long ago, two events occurred in our country that brought greater public attention to one of the lesser-known stories of World War II. President George W Bush awarded the Congressional Gold Medal, The highest civilian medal Congress can bestow, to four surviving members of the original 29 "wind talker"- Native Americans of the Navajo nation who served as Marines in the Pacific theater and who used their Navajo Language as a communications code the Japanese found impossible to break. At about the same time, a Hollywood motion picture names "Wind Talkers" was released, which gave a fact-based, but somewhat fictionalized account of the same story.

The word windtalkers refers to the Navajo way of speaking, a talking into the wind. A Navajo code talker was assigned to each Marine division to provide secure communication between them free from interception by the Japanese. In what undoubtedly sounded like mere gibberish to eavesdropping enemy, these "wind talkers" used their unique language to coordinate battle plans and strategy as well as call in artillery strikes. Significant contributions to the American victories on Guadalcanal, Iwo Jima, and other major battles on the islands of the Pacific were made.

This story of the Navajo windtalkers brought to my mind a connection with those believers long ago who talked into the "wind" of Pentecost. The Greek word "pneuma", which is often, translated "spirit," also means "breath" or "wind". The 120 believers gathered in the upper room heard "a sound from heaven, as of a rushing mighty wind," and they "began to speak with other tongues." These newly spirit-filled believers were spiritual "wind talkers" they spoke in a new language that was like a breath of Heaven.

Just as the Japanese could not penetrate the code of the Navajo windtalkers, so the devil cannot brake through the language of the Spirit. Speaking in tongues is a heavenly communication, a language that links us with the glory of God. It puts us in tune with His heart and mind. Just

as the Navajo windtalkers alone could understand each other in their unique communication, speaking in tongues is with the Lord, a special language or code that cannot be intercepted, understood, or subverted by the enemy".

This, "encouraging myself", prayer language, which I did to build my most holy faith, which means I must be praying the word of God in language I had no understanding of, was helping to make all things work together for my good. It was literally snatching the world out of my life and helping to grow up my spirit man. Like Peter, who spent time around Jesus, but under pressure he denied him, lied about being with him, cursed out inquisitive people and returned to old familiar habits, I needed a transforming experience that would empower me to become a dominator, a world overcomer. I needed the final ingredient that would lead me to an altared life. When the bible says, "pray without ceasing," it means to live a life that never stops communing with God. The spirit man is so alive and tuned in with the Father that it speaks as it walks. It says, "Look at me and you do see the Father". My praying in the Holy Spirit led me to that walk. It helped me with the other part of prayer that is often neglected. It is the listening portion. When the spirit man is built up, the flesh slowly but surely ceases to dominate. It listens more and life change happens at a more accelerated pace.

21 Days of Glory

It was not prayer alone that got me this "altared"; this under total submission to the will of God; this fully desirous of communing with God all day long about everything, life. Mark 9:17-29 (KJV), tells the story of a father who brought his son to the Disciples of Christ and they could not heal him. After much discussion and inquiring by the disciples, Jesus shared why they could not heal this boy. He said, "Some things only come by fasting and praying". The flesh must be overtaken by the spirit, by starving it. Starve the flesh, feed the spirit with Word and pray for revelation. This gives behavior-conquering power to you. My life has never been the same.

Fasting and praying have partnered to give me identification and integrity, language and lifestyle, tongues and temperament. They have helped me to speak into a new generation of my sons and daughters in the faith about the importance of **character before communication**. We should live the gospel then we can preach without words so that when we do use words, people will see them as the essence of who we are and not phony foreign learned speech that impresses masses and supports a carnal, enemy invaded lifestyle.

For 21 days I turned off the world of television, newspaper and radio. I shut the secular world completely off so I could hear from God. I cut out foods and drinks containing any body altering substance. I wanted to only be moved by the presence of God. Finally, I experienced true flesh submission. It was during this season that I met Bishop William Murphy Jr. and became reacquainted with Pastor Michael Shakespeare. They helped me enhance our intercessory prayer ministry by giving our people a new style of prayer, called by Mike Bickle of the International House of Prayer in Kansas City, Missouri, "The Harp and Bowl" style or "worship intercession". It made praying easier until it became habit without help of music or corporate body. As you grow in relationship with The Lord Jesus, you do not have to have mood enhancing elements to talk with him or listen to him. However, as you will hear later in the atmosphere setting of prayer, music is always a helpful tool when you can have it. Intimacy is sought, as you begin to understand the value of the relationship and you cannot bear long silence between you and God. You will neither ignore Him nor fail to speak with Him all day long. There will be a yearning, a thirsting for fellowship with Him that makes you talk with Him about everything going on in your life. This consistent communion transforms you into His likeness.

Bishop Wellington Boone notes in his book, *My Journey With God*, "...when you consecrate yourself you prepare yourself daily and diligently (Proverbs 8:17) to do everything God might call on you to do. As you seek God daily and study His Word, ask Him to purify your heart, change your motivations, and help you to become more like Jesus. As the Holy Spirit sheds light on the unholy areas of your life, ask God to perfect you and get you in shape for the battle to come in the unknown future".

This is the process by which one comes to live the "altared" life. It is a seeking after God for cleansing and development. It is an urgent desire to be like Him in word and deed and daily positioning ones self to hear His voice concerning, the "me I was born again to be". I agree totally with the powerful statement

Bishop Boone makes later in his writing, "If your life is an awesome testimony to the reality of God, people can live off of the substance of your dedication." That statement is the essence of what it means to live this "altared life". You then become the standard by which others live their life by, because they have not yet met Christ. You show them the model by becoming it. They should be able to follow us to the feet of Jesus where they in turn learn how to walk in their created worth and model Christ for another. It is called the process of being fruitful and multiplying after the God kind. It is what "altared life" people do. I made a decision not just to pray or to fast in season, when others called it or religiously practiced it. I desired to live an altared life; a prayer centered fasted life. What a challenge!

Transformed

I studied the word on every subject that challenged me as a Christian (drinking, smoking, marriage). I repented and began making private and public confessions about my ignorance, mistakes, sins and shame. I apologized to my church, my former spouse and vowed to help others stuck in the world I was stuck in, to see a model that they could emulate. My friends ran the gamut from ridicule to rejoicing. Some said they liked me better when I was drinking (they missed the party guy who hung out all night.) Some called my life boring (No Wine, Women, Profanity or Perversion.) Some cancelled preaching engagements and revivals, but I was finally at peace. I knew now what Paul felt like on the road to Damascus. The Lord spoke to me and said, "There are seasons in your life where you have to learn how to be alone with me. You can't go back to your old crowd they will not understand you. You are not where they are anymore and awkward will be the description of your fellowship with them. Neither will you be appreciated by a new crowd. They do not know you. Some of them have seen you, but they do not yet believe you are different. This is the "find a Father or Mentor" stage. Read Paul's conversion experience and see his alone time and mentoring time with Ananias (Acts 9). Hear the voice of God for clear direction on your alignments and assignments. You are now the altar. You are the place where people come near and see the Father. When you reach this stage people will worship when they are near you. They sense the need to pray. They have a sense of expectation that God is healing, helping and giving them hope. You and I must become the altar of proof that the Lord is good. You are the fruit of the spirit. You are the taste people experience. When they meet you, they should taste His presence and respond with ecstatic passion, *"O taste and see that the LORD is good..."* (Psalm 34:8 KJV).

When I read where Jesus said, in John 17 (KJV) "If ye had known me, ye should have known my Father also: and from henceforth ye know him, and have seen him". And Paul's statement in 1Corinthains 11:1, "Follow me as I follow Christ." I thought to myself, I want to be able to say that. I want my life to measure up to look like I am the spitting image of my Dad. I am the transformed offspring of a loving forgiving father. I owe Him. And just as when people saw Jesus coming, they drew near to him so they could receive what the Father wanted to give them; I desire to be that vessel.

It's Your Turn to Testify

If you are reading this book you are interested in altering (changing) your life to live the "altared" (prayer and fasted) life. As you read the following chapter you will develop that life. On the way there, take down these three suggestions that will lead you to this life that will warm your Daddy's heart when he sees you develop them. They are a summary of this chapter and a foretaste of the chapter to come.

(1) ***Purpose Filled Prayer***

> Meeting your needs prayer: Prayer that addresses your challenges, issues, sins and witness. A study of Scriptures helps with this. Find every scripture that deals with your issues.

(2) ***Principal Centered Passion***

> That I might know Him in His Fullness. Not to know of Him, but intimacy with Him that causes me to get a "God said", for every area of my life, truly making Him Lord. My life is guided by the word and not traditions. I have become an "it is written" you see me; you see His word made flesh.

(2) ***Crucified Flesh: A lifestyle of fasting***

I am continuously starving my passions and desires, so that my spirit man is always stronger than my flesh.

Well, let's go deeper shall we?

Chapter 2

"The Power of an 'Altared' Life"

2 Chronicles 7:11-14, *"11 When Solomon had finished the temple of the LORD and the royal palace, and had succeeded in carrying out all he had in mind to do in the temple of the LORD and in his own palace, 12 the LORD appeared to him at night and said: "I have heard your prayer and have chosen this place for myself as a temple for sacrifices. 13 "When I shut up the heavens so that there is no rain, or command locusts to devour the land or send a plague among my people, 14 if my people, who are called by my name, will humble themselves and pray and seek my face and turn from their wicked ways, then will I hear from heaven and will forgive their sin and will heal their land."*

We don't just do church, we are the church. I have met people in malls and have evangelized and invited them to church. I have heard it all, especially from this present generation. Many of them say, "Listen, I don't do church." I help them to come up with a new answer, because I don't do church either; I am the church. The church is not a building. The church is in the heart of the people. If the people in the building (especially in leadership) are not living proof of the resurrection of Jesus and His love, then the world sees church as a building of hypocrites. The church is the model in flesh of the life of Jesus, the living, breathing example of what the Father looks like. It is spending time with Him that makes us resemble Him.

In order for us to understand that, we have to understand what it means to have an altared life. I know when you initially hear an altared life; you hear 'alter' meaning a change. Undoubtedly a change is necessary and unavoidable when you develop an "altared" life. Temporarily the words alter and altar, for the sake of emphasis, may be very helpful. An altered/altared life is a changed life.

If I have a changed life, then I have gone through a transformation process. I had to make something different happen. Romans 12:1-2 (KJV) says, *"[1]I beseech you therefore, brethren, by the mercies of God, that ye present your bodies a living sacrifice, holy, acceptable unto God, which is your reasonable service. [2]And be not conformed to this world: but be ye transformed by the renewing of your mind, that ye may prove what is that good, and acceptable, and perfect, will of God."* Altered, does mean changed, transformed. As well, the altared life is the life that has been transformed, or has been changed, by the renewing of our minds. It is the process of staying in the presence of God so much that I develop the mind of Christ. The world taught us how to live life another kind of way. The world says, "Get all you can and can all you get." The world says, "There is a certain way that you achieve things in life and sometimes it's by hook or crook, by beating somebody down, by making sure you put people down so you can feel good about yourself." The world-system says, "I want to make sure I succeed on your shoulders." It has nothing to do with God. A transformed mind understands this; I do not have to treat you badly for me to be successful. I do not have to put you down in order for me to become successful. As a matter of fact, we are all in this together. There is a theology that says this, that in the beginning (what we read in Genesis) the darkness was the place where God had demoted Satan and there is chaos where he is boss. When God began to bring creation in the world and give man to the world, He put man on the earth so that he could oversee Satan and keep Satan under his feet; have dominion over him. What we did was give our dominion to him by letting him coerce us into hearing his voice over the voice of God. All of our lives have been fighting back for the dominion that was once already ours. In Christ, you have it back. The changed life is seeing life from God's eyesight. When you see life from God's perspective, you understand who you are. How do I get to that? It comes with the altared life; the life that is consumed with God through prayer.

I want you to get that. The altared life is not just a life that changed; it has to get changed in the right way and it is changed through having a life that is transformed with prayer, praise, worship and fasting. Life lived in the presence of God. That is the altared life.

The altared life is simply, a totally God focused life. It says I am about the business of pleasing God with everything that I do. In Philippians 3:10 {KJV} Paul says, *"That I may know him..."* Here is Paul, an apostle, who says, "That I may know him, and the power of his resurrection..." You are talking about a man who was a lawyer, a man who describes himself as, a "Hebrew of Hebrews". He says, "I came from the right side of the track. I grew up with the right teachers. I grew up understanding all of the laws. I knew how to dot every "I" and cross every "t". I am an important citizen." But he says, "My life is nothing but dung, manure, when I compare it to Christ and the relationship I have now." Let me ask you a question. What is most important to you in your life? I am not telling you that education is not important, but is it so important that I should walk around having to brag about me or do I brag about the one who made me? I appreciate what He has done in my life. I have spent time on my knees and on my face and in the word of God, because now I have declared in my life that if no other person in this world has a God-centered life, the world is going to have somebody at which to look. If no other church in your city would live for God, I mean a righteous-centered church; I mean a church that believes, we live according to the word of God and God is going to honor what we do, you and your church should do it. I made up in my mind that like Paul said in Philippians 3:10, *"That I may know Him and the power of his resurrection..."* If I know Him and the power of His resurrection, then that means that I also have to know him in crucifixion and in death. I also have to know what it is like to be crucified. Stop getting your feelings hurt all the time. Do you know that when somebody says something about you and you get your feelings hurt, it means that you are not low enough or your flesh hasn't died enough? When you have dead flesh, whatever people say about you is not going to kill you because you are already dead. You can't kill somebody who is already dead. When Paul says, "In the power of His resurrection," he is saying, I want to know that when

I get crucified and when I crucify myself; when I am buried under, that the anointing of God can raise me up. I want to know the power of His resurrection. I want to know that the same God, the same Father that saw Jesus go down in the grave and had the power to raise Him up, has the power to raise me up also.

When you have a Christ-centered life, a prayer-centered, intimate relationship with the Father, you do not live in anger. You understand that Friday might be here right now, the cross might be here right now, but Sunday is coming. Resurrection day is on the way. Behind every Good (or bad) Friday, Easter Sunday morning has to show up.

When you build an altar, something changes about your life. There is then a filling of power that happens in your life. 2 Chronicles 7:14 says, *"[14]Iif my people who are called by my name will humble themselves and pray and seek my face and turn from their wicked ways, then I will hear from heaven and will forgive their sin and will heal their land."* The scripture starts off by saying, *"if my people...then* (a conditional statement says, if you fulfill the first half, I will take care of the second half). *If my people, who are called by my name* (the inside crowd), *will humble themselves* (get low, crucify their own flesh and understand that I am in charge of their lives and they don't have to worry about anything just trust me) *and pray and seek my face* (not my hands if they will see things like I see things, hear things like I hear things, say what I say) *and turn from their wicked ways* (you can not see what God sees or hear what God hears, say what God says and then not turn from your wicked ways), *then will I hear from heaven and will forgive their sin* (in other words, God says, "I will see them as a righteous-remnant and every time I see righteousness, royalty comes to mind, every time I see righteousness my Son comes to mind) *and I will heal their land."*

When God talks about righteousness in the Old Testament, obviously Jesus had not shown up. In 2 Corinthians 5:21, Paul writes *"...that we might be made the righteousness of God in him."* Why would God have to make us righteous? Because we could not achieve it own our own. He said in essence, "I have seen you all try to follow the law and every one of you messed up." He further intimates, "I have seen you try to follow righteousness and you messed up, now I will sacrifice my Son. His blood over your life forgives you of your sins. You are now made the righteousness of God in and through your faith in Christ Jesus." That is taken care of. When you accept Jesus Christ as your Savior, Lord over your life, you are automatically made righteous even if you make another mistake. But now Romans 6:1 says, *"What shall we say then? Shall we continue in sin, that grace may abound?"* He is convincing us that we have to fight to live according to what we've been made.

Why? In Proverbs 11 we find out what the benefits of righteousness are. I challenge you to read it. What are the benefits of righteousness? There **_are_** benefits to living the righteous life. Not just being made righteous, but living righteously. Proverbs 11:3-6, 8, 10, *"³The integrity of the upright guides them, but the unfaithful are destroyed by their duplicity ⁴ Wealth is worthless in the day of wrath, but righteousness delivers from death. ⁵ The righteousness of the blameless makes a straight way for them, but the wicked are brought down by their own wickedness. ⁶ The righteousness of the upright delivers them, but the unfaithful are trapped by evil desires. ⁸ The righteous man is rescued from trouble, and it comes on the wicked instead ¹⁰ When the righteous prosper, the city rejoices; when the wicked perish, there are shouts of joy."* So if we are prospering, if we are coming alive, if we are living this thing, guess what? Your city has to prosper. Why? Because we are at the center of it all and whatever is at the center will blow out to the edges. The anointing starts at the head and flows down to the skirts (Psalm 132). Proverbs 11:9, 11, 18, says, *"⁹...but through knowledge the righteous escape. ¹¹ Through the blessing of the upright a city is exalted, but by the mouth of the wicked it is destroyed. ¹⁸ The wicked man earns deceptive wages, but he who sows righteousness reaps a sure reward."* This is not a gamble. Do you know what a gamble is? It is a chance. It might happen or it might not. We are not looking for gambles we are looking for investments. Righteousness is an investment. It is a sure thing. Proverbs 11:19-21, 23-25, 28, *"¹⁹The truly righteous man attains life, but he who pursues evil goes to his death. ²⁰ The LORD detests men of perverse heart but he delights in those whose ways are blameless. ²¹ Be sure of this: The wicked will not go unpunished, but those who are righteous will go free. ²³ The desire of the righteous ends only in good, but the hope of the wicked only in wrath ²⁴ One man gives freely, yet gains even more; another withholds unduly, but comes to poverty ²⁵ A generous man will* *prosper; he who refreshes others will himself be refreshed. ²⁸ Whoever trusts in his riches will fall, but the righteous will thrive like a green leaf. ³⁰ The fruit of the righteous is a tree of life, and he who wins souls is wise."*

In Genesis, the tree of life is what God told them not to bother. He said so because it was the thing that gave eternity to life. Man was not born to die in the beginning that is why he lived so long. But sin bought death into the world, so the fruit of righteousness is the tree of life. Therefore, righteousness brings forth life eternally. Righteousness extends life. Sometimes righteous people die early, but their name doesn't have to. Life eternal is not in your body but in your spirit. Life is in your spirit-man. Your body is only the thing that houses your spirit. Long after your body is gone; your spirit ought to be in the next generation and the next generation. Somebody is supposed to know that you lived on the earth long after you are gone.

Power has to come for life and dominion is being restored. Dominion takes confidence, faith to achieve anything in life. We get our dominion back, our authority back, when we live the altared life. We get our speaking power back, when we live an altared life.

Curses are then broken, curses that began in our father's and our grandfather's lives. When you live an altared life, their will come a time in your life when you get to a place where you can not just pray for yourself, but you feel compelled to pray for your father, "God I ask for forgiveness of his sins. I pray for my grandfather, because there are some things that they passed down to my generation that I see in me and some I cannot. *My grandfather drank bourbon. He passed that down to my uncle Michael and my uncle Michael, who lived with me passed it down to me. It missed my Mother but it got her brother. My grandfather never drank unless he smoked and he never smoked unless he drank. My grandfather died of a heart attack sitting in a bank. Many years he gave his body over to the enemy. Then when they told him he needed to give up certain stuff, he had a triple-bypass surgery. They told him that he had to cut some things out of his diet i.e. pork, salt. He said, "Listen, I have been eating this all these years and I cannot stop now." So, he died. He handed some stuff down from generation to generation. I have to at sometime asked God to forgive him, forgive my uncle Michael, and forgive me so that I do not pass that stuff to my sons and daughters.* Not only for the natural children, but what about in my spiritual inheritance. There were men in my life who taught me how to live that lifestyle as a preacher. Spiritually those things can be passed down to my sons and daughters in ministry as well as the church I pastor and the churches I oversee as a whole. As I pen these words It is painful to think that I went through a divorce in my life. Unfortunately I did not know how to truly be a man of God although I had all the appearances of one. I let myself down and began something that needed to be broken. You see, divorce can become a generational curse. So then the seed of struggling marriages that had the option of divorce would be in our whole church. But we had to break it. You cannot break it without an altared life. I can see what God is saying. I can hear God's voice all the time. What happens when I hear God's voice and see what God is saying all the time is that I live my life not according to my feelings, I live it according to faith. I am married today by faith, not be feelings. My faith is according to the word of God. I believe that if I set a standard in my house and live a righteous example, even if my wife is not doing what I feel is right at a given moment, she will see somebody (the real thing) and look to model it. I do not love my wife by my feelings. Why? It is because I discovered that feelings change. I then will love her one-minute and when she acts abnormally the next minute I change my feelings. This is why I do not love her by my feelings. I love her by faith. I believe that however she is acting today she will act different tomorrow, because God is in our house. I cover our house every day, so she has to change. I don't love her based on my feelings. I don't love my children by my feelings, especially my spiritual children, because sometimes they act crazy. If I loved them based on my feelings, I might "kick them to the curb". I love them by faith. I understand that God is working on them. I believe that God is going to extract a change in their life, because I am going to be the real thing in front of them. I learned to stop saying, "I love somebody today and then I can't love them tomorrow." Is that the love of the Father? "You made me angry, I don't love you anymore." My baby son says that. He is immature. Like I said, he is a baby. He has not grown to know the God kind of love yet. He loves based on feelings and what you do for him. Should I as a grown man love the same way? Sure I will if I am not grown up in the Faith. Have you ever thought about what would happen if God decided to love you by feelings or by how you responded to what He asked you to do? It has been two years and you haven't gotten it done yet and God decided, "I'm sick of this mess, I don't love you anymore." If he loved you based on whether you are a consistent tither. He says, "Oh you are not going to help the body of Christ, then I don't love you." What if He loved you based upon whether you are speaking to Jane or not? If He decided, "I want to do this based on my feelings too." God offers an unconditional love in spite of you. Romans 5:8; *"while we were yet sinners, Christ died for us."* He died for the ungodly and He tells us, the righteous-remnant, "Don't model the world's way, model my way." You cannot do that without an altared life.

When you live a God-centered life, dominion is restored and curses are broken. It is like getting power back on after a storm. There will be redeeming qualities. Mark 9 shows us that when Jesus showed up the crowd turned and began to follow Him. Is there anybody following you? When you show up, Jesus ought to be showing up. Can you say like Paul in 1 Corinthians 11:1, *"Follow me as I follow Christ?"* When you live an altared life somebody is going to want to follow you around to see if they can experience the same thing you are experiencing. You will not have to ask them to come to church, they will be asking you, "Where do you go to worship? I want some coaching like that. I want my life to change like that." When they enter your church, it will be a 2 Chronicles 7:1 experience all over again. The glory was so thick that the priest couldn't even come in. No personality was allowed to be in the room. Confusion had to stop at the door. Egos had to be checked at the door.

The altared life is more than just a faith-statement. It is really about a life that has really been transformed and redirected by God. A life lived on His principles and practices.

Let's look at 2 Chronicles 7:11-14, when Solomon had finished the temple; let me put it another way, when the wise man had finished the house that belonged to God, when this wise man had finished building the house that belonged to God, something happened. I want you to expect something awesome when you finish building your house, (you are the temple of God). When Solomon built the royal palace and had succeeded in carrying out all that he had in mind to do with the temple of the Lord, and in his own place, the Lord did something. He appeared. The Lord will show up if you give Him your place. 2 Chronicles 7:12, *"¹²the LORD appeared to him at night and said: "I have heard your prayer.* Can I suggest this? If you have not built this place, your life, for Him, then the opposite is so. Then He does not hear your prayer. How does He hear prayer from a house that is not His residence? He said *"and have chosen this place for myself as a temple for sacrifices"; u*nderstand that sacrifices were for the purpose of worship. *"I have chosen this place where worship can be seen, where the love of God can go on. I have chosen this place where my voice can be heard, where victory can be seen, where life-changed can be seen. I have chosen this place of sacrifice. I have chosen this place as altar so that when people see it they will worship me."* Now, when people come into your presence, they experience God. God has chosen you as a temple of sacrifice, of worship. I'll ask the question again, is anybody following you? Is your life worth following? What happens to people when they follow you? If they become like you, will they become like the Father? He has chosen your life as a sacrifice to him. Verse 13 and 14 leaves the earth's wholeness in the hands of the altared people. "I will come and dwell where worship happens." When I shut up heaven and everything else closes down on the earth and the earth cannot see the blessings of God, *if my people who are called by name, if they will humble themselves and pray and seek my face and turn from their wicked ways, then I will hear from heaven, I will forgive them of their sins then I will heal the land.* God puts the condition of healing for your city and the world in the hand of His people (You). So, if it doesn't change it is our fault. Have you ever wondered why the liquor stores stay open? Do you ever wonder why the drug dealer stays in business? He said, "If my people will turn around, whatever Heaven has shut down I will send healing." You have to read further down to 2 Chronicles 7:15-16, *"¹⁵Now my eyes will be open and my ears attentive to the prayers offered in this place. ¹⁶I have chosen and consecrated this temple so that my Name may be there forever. My eyes and my heart will always be there."* Can anybody see that you are the one keeping the family of earth together?

There are three things that I want to give you so you can see that you are why this book was written.

1. To show you:

   The <u>promised you</u>. God has assigned me to share with you the pathway to the promised you. There is a place that you were born to be, that you may not have arrived there yet. The chapters that follow will help you head in the right direction so you can get to that place. It is your destiny. There is a vision that God has for you individually and there is also a vision that God has for you as a part of your local and corporate body of Christ. God wants you to focus in on what He wants you to do in His Kingdom. He wants to show you the promised you. One problem always surfaces. It is not one that cannot be overcome.

2. To show you:

   <u>There is a pull of the enemy</u>. You are now a target for enemy attack. The Devil's job is to obscure, to blind us from seeing the place that God has promised for our lives. He works over time to do just that. If you get in the presence of the Lord daily and often you will never fear the enemy but you will cherish the fact that he thinks so much of your anointing that he would dare use so much energy trying to circumvent your authority. He actually fears your future when you are close to the Father.
   Satan will major at offering you invitations to things that keeps you from your potential. Hebrews 12:1, says, *"Therefore, since we are surrounded by such a great cloud of witnesses, let us throw off everything that hinders and the sin that so easily entangles, and let us run with perseverance the race marked out for us."* You have to put the weight off first. You cannot run when you have a bunch of weight on you. I am not talking about just physical weight. Has anybody ever tried to run or walk with ankle-weights on? It is harder to run or walk like that. On the other hand, do you know they also make you faster? Note this however; they don't make you faster until you take them off. That is how it is with our burdens. That is how it is with our sins. They weigh us down and slow us down in route to our destiny, until we take them off. What you were able to do before you took on those sins, now you can do them faster better. Why? It seems like you should do them at the same pace, but no, the sins are gone now. When you shake them off, the weight is gone. When weight is on you build up strength. You now have become stronger, wiser, better. You can run faster,

jump higher and endure more. You can hear His voice clearer and that alone will make a difference. The altared life will change the way you see and hear which ultimately changes the way you do. Now I know I can run to my destiny In Hebrews 12:2says, *"Let us fix our eyes on Jesus...* (The promise)*"* The enemy always has a pull. I am here to remind you of that pull and to let you know that his pull is not a burden when you stay close. You expect it and learn to laugh even when the pressure is on because you know the end result. Always live with the understanding that the last word over your life is, "more than conqueror", "world overcomer", "and dominator", unless you change it.

As I previously stated, the altared life, the life lived in the presence of God thru prayer and fasting, is Satan's greatest fear. You become a weapon against him every where you go. Come, let us get ready to defeat the enemy together. This is going to be a rewarding journey. There is a champion in you that just needs some coaching. Is that not what the story of the children of Israel is really all about? Out of Egypt into the dessert and that is really when the coaching starts. There are some folks that it takes a long time to get them out of Egypt. For some of us it just takes a while to get us convinced that we do not need "Egypt" stuff any more in our life. We have been in Egypt so long. "I have been doing it this way so long. Some people admit, "I don't know any other way to live. I have been lying all my life so lying is a part of my character. If you want me to stop lying I have to stop living or die." Die? That is really what the past is about. It is about getting you to die. Sometimes in order for you to die, you have to cry. It is a sign of immaturity. It is a trait of children. Children cry when something they feel precious is taken away from them, because they do not understand that something greater is on the way. Sometimes we have to go through our childhood of crying before we can grow up and experience the fullness of God. Egypt is tough and so is the desert (the journey to the promised place of God). Often the desert experience is difficult because I am out of Egypt (bondage) physically, but I keep looking back, therefore I still live there in my mind.

You are the Moses of your own destiny, but you need confidence to arrive there. Moses had a problem. When God called Moses, Moses said, "I am not a man of good speech." He was really telling God, "I don't have confidence to lead anybody anywhere." In other words he was saying, "I don't know if I have the stuff inside of me to fulfill the assignment that you have placed on my life." Have you ever asked yourself if God would ever call you, give you a destiny, or assign you to a task, if He had not already equipped you to perform it? He will never give you an assignment that He has not already equipped you to accomplish. What you need now is the confidence, the faith to get it done. I want to tell you who I am as you read this. I call myself your Aaron. Here is the revelation. Aaron was Moses' priest. He was his brother as well. He was called to speak to Pharaoh because Moses lacked confidence in his own abilities.

God has called me to be your priest, your coach to help you speak to your Pharaohs until you can do it on your own. God calls Aaron to speak to the Pharaohs in the lives of the people of God, because the lead person (you are the lead person of your destiny) didn't have the confidence to get it done themselves. Until you are strong enough to speak on your own, I will always be here. This book is your guide to freedom. The great thing is this, you will not need me the same way you need me as time goes on. As you keep studying this book and the chapters to come, you will be able to lead your own life as well as your family, in prayer. You will not wait until a *fast* is called. You will call a fast for yourself when you know that there are issues of the flesh that you or your family has to overcome. In time (as you grow in your understanding of the heart of the Father), your prayer and fasting will move to things your city or nation has to overcome. Now you come to the place where you live an altared life.

One final note before we make this journey.

When you are in the desert, your past will pursue you until you no longer fear that it has strength to rule you. The rest of this book is about how you can experience victories along the way. Many Christians live their whole lives in misery. They carry burdens they were not supposed to carry. While it is true we have to be in battle while on the earth, it is clear to me in the word of God that the battles are perfunctory tasks as overseers of the enemy. He tries to lift up his ugly head in intimidation, as though he has rights. When we do not know who we are in Christ, then the devil laughs and takes ground in our lives that he has no right to. We were born to have dominion, be fruitful and multiply. We must keep the revealed word in us so that Satan knows that there is no win on his side when it comes to us. Read Exodus 17 where the children of Israel fought the Amalekites. That was not in the Promise Land, it was on the way to the Promised Land. You can experience victories on the way to heaven. Those victories are designed to keep you encouraged at least. They are reminders of your proper place in the earth. Stop giving Satan your position of authority. Now lets go kick some devil posterior by learning how to access the power of God within us. Your life is getting ready to be altared. Get excited! The whole earth has been groaning waiting for this moment. This is the moment of your elevation to "SONSHIP". It's not about your gender, but Christ in you for the world to see. I am ecstatic to play a small part in it. Come on, let's go higher.

Chapter 3

"Preparation for the Journey"

In the opening words of Chapter 3 of Samuel E. Balentine's book entitled "Prayer in the Hebrew Bible: The Drama of Divine-Human Dialogue", he comments on the first four words of the bible which says, "In the beginning God…" He says, "With these words the Hebrew bible presents a confessional perspective that shapes all that follows: "In the Beginning God. Whatever criteria one uses to define prayer, prayer is also, perhaps especially shaped by this confession. All prayer is directed to God."

When a person prays, he or she is acknowledging the author, creator of the universe as one to be respected. We are to continue to relate to Him as the one who is powerful enough to direct and redirect life. According to the book of Ecclesiastes chapter 3 verse 11, God has created man with a longing for relationship with Him. There is no real fulfillment or satisfaction that humanity can find until it acknowledges that we are creatures of purpose and that finding our purpose is connected to continuous communion with God through his son Jesus Christ. Prayer is that way of communion. It is learning how to speak to and agree with God. It is listening to his voice and confirming the directions by the spirit of His work, neither swaying to the left or right.

The aftermath of prayer should be that a person is now fully clothed or re-clothed with the glory of God. According to Exodus, after Moses met with God, he had to veil his face because the glory was so strong upon him. Can that be said about us? When we finish praying does the glory appear?

Speaking of the glory, we listed in the previous chapter concerning II Chronicles chapters 5-7, where we find Solomon's prayer at the dedication of the temple, resulted in all flesh diminishing. The bible declares that the priest could not even enter the temple. When RIGHT prayer is offered, it burns away all flesh: worldly desires; lusts; personalities; egos; flawed feelings or whatever is unlike God. A singleness of purpose surfaces, gifts and fruits for service of the kingdom are highlighted. Praise, worship and joy are now evidenced in our face, hands, heart and tongue.

I Kings 8:22-53 offers to us Solomon's prayer at the dedication of the temple.

Some suggest that it is a prayer about the temple that suggests it is the "place to offer prayer", because it was to be God's dwelling place as well. However, according to New Testament scripture, a change occurs.

I Corinthians 3:16-17, [16]Don't you know that you yourselves are God's temple and that God's Spirit lives in you? [17]If anyone destroys God's temple, God will destroy him; for God's temple is sacred, and you are that temple.

I Corinthians 6:19, do you not know that your body is a temple of the Holy Spirit, who is in you, whom you have received from God? You are not your own;

We have become God's dwelling place. If we are the temple of the Holy Spirit, then prayers ought to be offered in us. Then should not the same result of the glory coming occur?

This chapter is a step-by-step look at the tabernacle found in the Old Testament. While the tabernacle is a place that we can model prayer for the purpose of developing the "altared" life, it is imperative to see Christ and His presence in every piece of furniture. The primary focus of this chapter is not brick mortar, wood, metal, wax, veils or scents, but to glorify, exalt and worship Christ the Lord.

A walk through the temple would give to us the six significant areas in which we will focus our attention on as we help guide you to a meaningful, productive prayer life. Each area has a function in preparing you for experiencing the presence of God daily and often, not just on Sundays. Read through these carefully so you gain an understanding of what you are doing and why you are doing it, while you pray.

The Replica (of the temple)

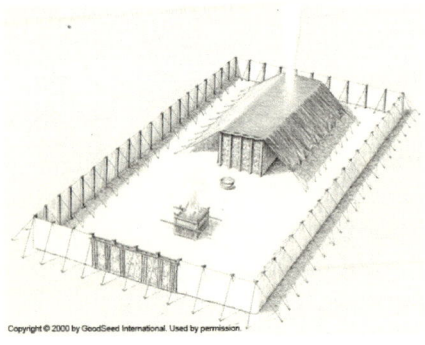

The Brazen Altar

The brazen altar, bronze altar or altar of sacrifice was positioned right inside the courtyard upon entering the gate to the tabernacle. The Hebrew root for altar means, "To slay" or "slaughter." The Latin word Alta means "high." An altar is a "high place for sacrifice or slaughter." The altar stood raised on a mound of earth, higher than its surrounding furniture. This is a projection of Christ, our sacrifice, lifted up on the cross, His altar, which stood on a hill called Golgotha. The altar was made of wood from the acacia tree and overlaid with bronze (usually symbolic of judgment on sin in the Bible), measuring 7.5 feet on all four sides and 4.5 feet deep. Four horns projected from the top four corners and a bronze grating was inside to hold the animal. Although the blood of the sacrifices covered over the sins of the Israelites, they had to perform the sacrifices year after year, for they were

Brazen Altar

not freed permanently of a guilty conscience. However, Jesus Christ, the Lamb of God came as the ultimate and last sacrifice for mankind when He offered up His life. As Isaiah prophesied, the Christ would be like a lamb that is led to slaughter and pierced for our transgressions. His blood was sprinkled and poured out at the cross for us. In a later chapter we will pray in thanksgiving for the cleansing, healing, delivering, curse breaking power of the blood over our lives. Genesis 9:4 tells us that "life is in the blood". Our life is restored, resurrected in the blood of Jesus. The brazen altar represents a place of sacrifice. It represents a place to die to the flesh; a place of arresting the worldly in us and rising up the righteousness. It is the place of removing the curses of iniquity and its penalties, which include poverty and eternal death and replacing it with a "Deut. 28: 1-14" life, the life of blessings, forever.

The Laver

The laver, or basin, was a large bowl filled with water located halfway between the brazen altar and the Holy Place. Although God did not give specific measurements for the Laver, it was to be made entirely of bronze. The priests were to wash their hands and their feet in it before entering the Holy of Holies. The laver was located in a convenient place for washing and stood as a reminder that people need cleansing before approaching God. The priests atoned for their sins through a sacrifice at the brazen altar, but they cleansed themselves at the laver before serving in the Holy Holies, so that they would be pure and not die before a holy God.

As believers we are forgiven through Christ's work on the cross, but we are washed through His Word. We need to be washed daily in His Word to cleanse ourselves, so that we can serve and minister before Him. [1] Just as we cleanse the outer body with water so that we smell fresh and clean, we need inward cleansing daily also. Ephesians 5:26b talks about the washing by the word. The blood and the word in prayer is a daily inward cleansing process. Not just a Sunday religious ritual. To represent Christ in the world we must offer our lives clean. II Corinthians 2:15 tells us that "we are the fragrance of life". The laver cleanses us before approaching God, as well as gets us ready to be ambassadors for him in the world.

The Golden Candlestick

This was the first room in the tent of the tabernacle. There were three pieces of furniture in the Holy Place: the golden candlestick or menorah, the table of showbread and the golden altar of incense. The golden candlestick stood at the left side of the Holy of Holies. It was hammered out of one piece of pure gold. The lamp stand had a central branch from which three branches extended from each side, forming a total of seven branches. Seven lamps holding olive oil and wicks stood on top of the branches. Each branch looked like that of an almond tree, containing buds, blossoms and flowers. The priests were instructed to keep the lamps burning continuously. (Leviticus *24:1-3)*

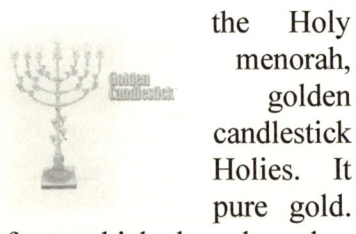

Jesus is represented by the main branch of the lamp stand and we, as believers, are represented by the six branches that extend from the original branch. The branches serve as a picture of Jesus' description of our relationship with him: "I am the vine, you are the branches ... apart from me you can do nothing" (John 15:5). [1]

This area where the Golden Candlestick with its ever-burning flame, represents the place the Holy Spirit plays in your life. He is the keeper of the flame. An illuminating presence, that never lets you walk in darkness, because He dwells in you. His presence opens the eyes of your understanding in ever area of life. He is the author of wisdom, knowledge, counsel and power, which enables you to conquer the world. You are actually more than a conqueror. You are a world overcomer. That confidence abides when He has full permission to lead and guide you.

The Shewbread

The table of shewbread was a small table made of acacia wood and overlaid with pure gold. It measured 3 feet by 1.5 feet and was 2 feet, 3 inches high. It stood on the right side of the Holy Place across from the lamp stand and held 12 loaves of bread, representing the 12 tribes of Israel. The priests baked the bread with fine four and it remained on the table before the Lord for a week; every Sabbath day the priests would remove it and eat it in the Holy Place, then put fresh bread on the table. Only priests could eat the bread, and it could only be eaten in the Holy Place, because it was holy. The Shewbread was also called "bread of the presence", because it was to always be in the Lord's presence. The table and the bread were a picture of God's willingness to fellowship and commune (literally speaking, sharing something in common) with man. It was like an invitation to share a meal, an extension of friendship. Eating together often is an act of fellowship. God was willing for man to enter into His presence to fellowship with Him and this invitation was always open.

As you will see in Chapter 6, the bread of life represents the word of God. We are called to honor, to live, to teach and to pray the word of God. Man cannot live by man-made bread alone. He was born to live off of "A God Said". The word is bread for our spirit man. The spirit in us is what will live for eternity. The body, which lives off of physical bread lives in years, but will eventually die. It only houses the spirit while it fulfils its earthly assignment. Therefore, everyday should be a bread (word) eating day. Whatever we eat we should use to confess for the rest of the day, thereby nourishing our spiritual bodies off of that same bread all day. How do you spell world-class spiritual body?

The Incense Altar

The golden altar of incense sat in front of the curtain that separated the Holy Place from the Holy of Holies. This altar was smaller than the brazen altar. It was a square with each side measuring 1.5 feet and was 3 feet high. It was made of acacia wood and overlaid with pure gold. Four horns

31

protruded from the four corners of the altar. God commanded the priests to burn incense on the golden altar every morning and evening at the same time that the daily burnt offerings were made. The incense was to be left burning continually throughout the day and night as a pleasing aroma to the Lord. It was made of an equal part of four precious spices and was considered holy. The incense was a symbol of the prayers and intercession for the people going up to God as a sweet fragrance. God wanted His dwelling to be a place where people could approach Him and pray to Him.

The incense altar is the place of praise or appreciation for what God has done. Psalm 22:3 says, He inhabits, or comes to rest with us as we praise Him. As overcomer worshippers, we fill the room with fragrance in the nostrils of our Father. The song writer said it like this, "I will enter his gates with thanksgiving in my heart. I will enter his court with praise. I will say this is the day that the Lord Has mad, I will rejoice for you have me glad. As a song-writer, I penned these words, "You are Healer, Sanctifier, Provider, You Are My Everything. You are Victory, Peace, Ever Present, You Are My Everything."

The Holy of Holies and the Veil

Within the Holy Place of the tabernacle, there was an inner room called the Holy of Holies, or the Most Holy Place. It was a most sacred room, a place no ordinary person could enter. It was God's special dwelling place in the midst of His people. During the Israelites' wanderings in the wilderness, God appeared as a pillar of cloud or fire in and above the Holy of Holies. The Holy of Holies was a perfect cube; its length, width and height were all equal to 15 feet.

A thick curtain separated the Holy of Holies from the Holy Place. This curtain, known as the "veil," was made of fine linen and blue, purple and scarlet yarn. The word "veil" in Hebrew means a screen, divider or separator that hides. What was this curtain hiding? Essentially, it was shielding a holy God from sinful man. Whoever entered into the Holy of Holies was entering the very presence of God. In fact, anyone except the high priest who entered the Holy of Holies would die. Even the high priest, God's chosen mediator with His people, could only pass through the veil and enter this sacred dwelling once a year, on a prescribed day called the Day of Atonement.

The picture of the veil was that of a barrier between man and God. God's eyes are too pure to look on evil and He can tolerate no sin (Habakkuk 1:13). The veil was a barrier to make sure that man could not carelessly and irreverently enter into God's awesome presence. Even as the high priest entered the Holy of Holies on the Day of Atonement, he had to make some meticulous preparations. He had to wash himself, put on special clothing, bring burning incense to let the smoke cover his eyes from a direct view of God, and bring blood with him to make atonement for sins.

So the presence of God remained shielded from man behind a thick curtain during the history of Israel. However, Jesus' sacrificial death on the cross changed that. When He died, the curtain in the Jerusalem temple was torn in half, from the top to the bottom. As the veil was torn, the Holy of Holies was exposed. God's presence was now accessible to all. Jesus' death has atoned for our sins and made us right before God. The torn veil illustrated Jesus' body broken for us, opening the way for us to come to God. As Jesus cried out "It is finished!" on the cross, He was indeed proclaiming that God's redemptive plan was now complete. The age of animal offerings was over. The ultimate offering had been sacrificed. We can now boldly enter into God's presence, "the inner sanctuary behind the curtain, where Jesus, who went before us, has entered on our behalf." Hebrews 6:19-20, "19We have this hope as an anchor for the soul, firm and secure. It enters the inner sanctuary behind the curtain, 20where Jesus, who went before us, has entered on our behalf. He has become a high priest forever, in the order of Melchizedek."

The Ark of the Covenant

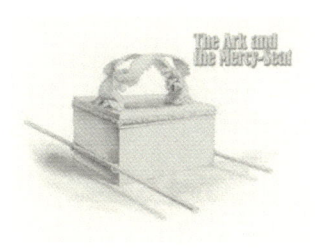

Within the Holy of Holies, shielded from the eye of the common man, was one piece of furniture comprising of two parts: the Ark of the Covenant and the atonement cover (or "mercy seat") on top of it. The ark was a chest made of acacia wood, overlaid with pure gold inside and out. It was 3 feet, 9 inches long and 2 feet, 3 inches wide and high. God commanded Moses to put in the ark three items: a golden pot of manna, Aaron's staff that had budded, and the two stone tablets on which the Ten Commandments were written. The atonement cover was the lid for the ark. On top of it stood two cherubim (angels) at the two ends, facing each other. The cherubim, symbols of God's divine presence and power, were facing downward toward the ark with outstretched wings that covered the atonement cover. The whole structure was beaten out of one piece of pure gold. The atonement cover was God's dwelling place in the tabernacle. It was His throne, flanked by angels. God appeared in His glory in "unapproachable light" (1 Timothy 6:16). This light is sometimes referred to as the Shekinah glory. The word Shekinah has the same roots as the word for tabernacle in Hebrew and refers to the presence of the Lord.

Because the ark was God's throne among His people, it was a symbol of His presence and power with them wherever it went. Yet the ark could not be treated with irreverence because it was also a symbol of God's judgment and wrath.

These three articles were preserved in the ark throughout Israel's history as an unpleasant symbol of man's sins and shortcomings, a reminder of how they rejected God's provision, authority and right standard of living. It pointed to man as a helpless sinner.

It may have been uncomfortable to think that God's splendor was so close to the three articles associated with man's sinfulness. But this is where God's provision comes in. When God looked down from His presence above the ark, He did not see the reminders of sin. They were covered by a necessary object — the atonement cover.

Every year, the high priest would enter the Holy of Holies on the Day of Atonement. Bringing burning incense to shield his eyes from a direct view of God's glory, he sprinkled blood from a bull onto the atonement cover for his and his household's sins, then sprinkled blood from a goat for all the sins of Israel. God promised that when He saw the blood, it would cover over man's sin. (To atone for means to cover over). God did not see the sin anymore, but the provision instead, and it appeased His wrath.

Jesus Christ has become our permanent atonement, cover. Through Jesus' blood, our sins have been covered over. When God looks at us, He doesn't see our sin, but the provision: His own Son. Jesus laid down His life for us as an innocent sacrifice so that God would look on us and see His perfection.

The atonement cover was God's throne in the midst of the Israelites. God is on His throne today in heaven and Jesus, our high priest, is at His right side. When we come to God now, we approach a throne of grace.

"Let us then approach the throne of grace with confidence, so that we may receive mercy and find grace to help us in our time of need." (Hebrews 4:16)

Chapter 4

"The Traps of the Enemy"

II Corinthians 10: 4, 5 (AMP) 4For the weapons of our warfare are not physical [weapons of flesh and blood], but they are mighty before God for the overthrow and destruction of strongholds, 5[Inasmuch as we] refute arguments and theories and reasoning and every proud and lofty thing that sets itself up against the [true] knowledge of God; and we lead every thought and purpose away captive into the obedience of Christ (the Messiah, the Anointed One),

The Bible can be called many things. One of them would be the Warfare Manual. A part of prayer is called warfare. If we are not prepared to battle the enemy, we are in trouble. The word of God is clear. The enemy is under our feet. He is a defeated foe, but constantly we are taught to fight the good fight of faith. The sixth chapter of Ephesians teaches us to put the whole armor of God on so that we can fight. One of the pieces is the shield of faith. That piece is to reflect every fiery dart the enemy throws. If our faith is strong then we can fight with it. Weak faith is an open door to fear. Fear is "an agitated feeling aroused by awareness of danger or trouble; an uneasy feeling that something may happen contrary to one's desires; to be uneasy or apprehensive over an unpleasant possibility."[7] So then to operate by faith we must hear the Word of God consistently and believe it. To walk confidently by faith we must know that the promises of the one who we have faith in are true. To truly believe the promises, it is essential to intimately know *"the Promiser"*. In order to know Him intimately, prayer is essential. The more you pray, the more you will praise and worship. This will increase the intimacy and cause a hunger for the Word, which will fuel the faith to live. The chief aim of the adversary is to stop you from those intimate encounters with the eternal God.

In this chapter I want to spell out five things that Satan uses to interrupt your intimacy or to hinder you from getting there period: Unworthiness, Ignorance, Fear of Failure, Fatigue, and Pressure.

Unworthiness

How many people who are Christians still see themselves as "filthy rags" instead of ambassadors, chosen generation, royal priesthood or righteousness of God? Many children of God have weak prayer lives. Satan causes us to see our shame and relive a, "Adam in the garden", scene. After Adam sinned he hid from God, as if God could not tell that something was wrong. Lack of communion was a sign that sin had entered into the life of Adam. It made Adam feel unworthy to go into the presence of God. And while it should, he still must go, so as to become clean, healed and delivered from his sins.

One of the tricks of the enemy is to get us to be out of communion with our Father. When we do that, we lose the ability to know the sound of His voice. When we cannot hear His voice we cannot speak as He speaks nor obey what He says. Thus we live in a state of curses rather than blessings. Proverbs 18:21 tells us that *"Death and life are in the power of the tongue: and they that love it shall eat the fruit thereof"*.

If we cannot hear life from the giver of life, how can we have faith to speak life? If we cannot speak it, then we die. We lose the power to live. We lose the breath God gives that provides joy and strength to our existence.

For years in my personal life I felt unworthy to pray because of a dual lifestyle. I knew that I could ask for help to preach because people needed it, but for personal needs I felt shame and guilt would exclude me from an audience with God. Yet it was that very shame and guilt that a father desires a son to bring before him in repentance, so that the son can begin to experience the benefits of the relationship and all the healing, deliverance and peace that accompanies it.

Listen carefully: NEVER let Satan convince you that you are too unworthy to talk to your own father. It is a trap. Run to Him! He is waiting, Prodigal Child. The dirty, smelly, empty, broken, and broke all must run to Him. His healing, forgiving arms of love wait without condemnation or criticism.

Ignorance

Genesis 1:26-28

^{26}Then God said, "Let us make man in our image, in our likeness, and let them rule over the fish of the sea and the birds of the air, over the livestock, over all the earth, and over all the creatures that move along the ground." ^{27} So God created man in his own image, in the image of God he created him; male and female he created them. ^{28} God blessed them and said to them, "Be fruitful and increase in number; fill the earth and subdue it. Rule over the fish of the sea and the birds of the air and over every living creature that moves on the ground."

Psalms 8:4-5

^{4} what is man that you are mindful of him, the son of man that you care for him? ^{5} You made him a little lower than the heavenly beings and crowned him with glory and honor.

Genesis 2:17

but you must not eat from the tree of the knowledge of good and evil, for when you eat of it you will surely die.

I Corinthians 15:22

For as in Adam all die, so in Christ all will be made alive.

II Corinthians 4:4

The god of this age has blinded the minds of unbelievers, so that they cannot see the light of the gospel of the glory of Christ, who is the image of God.

Neil Anderson in his book "Victory over Darkness", begins chapter one with a very important question," Who are you?" Anderson indicates that who we are has nothing to do with our position, our residence, our denomination, our weight, height, or age. It is determined by what we do. He says, "Your understanding of who God is and who you are in relationship to Him is the entire foundation for your belief system and your behavior patterns as a Christian." Therefore it is critical for every child of God to acquire as much knowledge as they can, early and often in their Christian walk. Knowledge is power. Knowledge about the wrong things produces power to do evil. Knowledge about God is the power to walk as an heir. Everything He has belongs to his children. You, dear friend, are one of his children.

When Adam and Eve experienced the fall, they lost their sense of direction. They meandered through the garden hoping not to be discovered for their nakedness. They lost their spiritual covering. They lost their "God coat." They lost knowledge of who they were. Genesis 3: 11 (Amp) records the question God raised to them. "Who told you that you were naked?" When we lose communion with God, we lose knowledge of who we are. Satan hates to see us praying because he knows information, direction, and strength for our journey comes from it.

There are five passages of scripture that I want to share with you so that ignorance, or lack of knowledge, does not steal from your ability to succeed at fulfilling your birthright as a dominator in the kingdom of God.

(1) This is who you are:

Genesis 1: 26-28

[26] *Then God said, "Let us make man in our image, in our likeness, and let them rule over the fish of the sea and the birds of the air, over the livestock, over all the earth, and over all the creatures that move along the ground."* [27] *So God created man in his own image, in the image of God he*

created him; male and female he created them. ²⁸ *God blessed them and said to them, "Be fruitful and increase in number; fill the earth and subdue it. Rule over the fish of the sea and the birds of the air and over every living creature that moves on the ground."*

This passage establishes for us our ancestry. We see our bloodline. We understand that we have the DNA of the creator of the universe. The power of God is in us and has given us the ability to produce after his own kind.

(2)   This is how God sees you:

Psalms 8: 4- 5

⁴ *what is man that you are mindful of him, the son of man that you care for him?* ⁵ *You made him a little lower than the heavenly beings and crowned him with glory and honor.*

This passage helps us see our created worth through the eyes of a worshipper. David was a prayer warrior, a persistent worshipper, and therefore received a revelation of who he was and who he was created to be in spite of his failures. The picture of our image of God person should always be before us, to inspire us to attain the position where we were birthed.

(3)   This is what appeared to you:

Genesis 2: 17

"but you must not eat from the tree of the knowledge of good and evil, for when you eat of it you will surely die."

(4)   This is the pathway to return:

Romans 6:16 (AMP)

Do you not know that if you continually surrender yourselves to anyone to do his will, you are the slaves of him whom you obey, whether that be to sin, which leads to death, or to obedience which leads to righteousness (right doing and right standing with God)?

(5) This is the position you are returning to:

Galatians 3:13-15

[13]Christ redeemed us from the curse of the law by becoming a curse for us, for it is written: "Cursed is everyone who is hung on a tree." [14]He redeemed us in order that the blessing given to Abraham might come to the Gentiles through Christ Jesus, so that by faith we might receive the promise of the Spirit. [15]Brothers let me take an example from everyday life. Just as no one can set aside or add to a human covenant that has been duly established, so it is in this case.

Galatians 3:26-29

[26]You are all sons of God through faith in Christ Jesus, [27]for all of you who were baptized into Christ have clothed yourselves with Christ. [28]There is neither Jew nor Greek, slave nor free, male nor female, for you are all one in Christ Jesus. 29If you belong to Christ, then you are Abraham's seed, and heirs according to the promise.

Prosperity is the result of the blessing of Abraham. The blessing of Abraham is our material inheritance, in contrast to, the blessing of David, which is our spiritual inheritance. Galatians 4:1 indicates to us that with out spiritual maturity, no matter what is in our account we cannot access it.

Galatians 4:1 says, *"What I am saying is that as long as the heir is a child, he is no different from a slave, although he owns the whole estate".*

As much as I love my 2-year-old son, if I give him an inheritance, say a $10,000 seed. In his hands it has no value to him. In Darryl's hand, it is colored on, torn up, placed in his mouth-eaten (seed eaten) or thrown away like his mom's cell phone. He doesn't know the value. It is up to me, and my wife to teach him that value. Then he can be trusted with it.

Prayer postures us for instruction. Instruction renders us knowledgeable. Knowledge received and acted wisely upon is power. When we know who we are, our purpose, and the plans God has for us, then the next trick or trap is exposed and laughed about.

Fear of Failure

Of course, this trap is tied to the trap labeled "unworthy". One of the tricks of Satan is to convince us that when we have had failures in the pursuit of holiness, then we should not even attempt to pray. While I agree that our best results in the area of manifested blessings comes with righteous living, I also know that true repentance washes away the sins of the past. And while some may have to face some natural worldly penalties for actions done in the flesh, our father is ready to dispatch angels *(Hebrews 1:14, "Are not all angels ministering spirits sent to serve those who will inherit salvation")* to minister to us or help us with whatever we need, because of our imputed righteousness.

Prayer brings me to a place of trust in God where I begin to see myself as a truly loved child that makes requests of a father and awaits his loving provision. I must therefore, understand my Father's heart. He desires my requests and long to respond. Matthew 7:7-11 (NASB) [7]*"Ask, and it will be given to you; seek, and you will find; knock, and it will be opened to you.* [8]*"For everyone who asks receives, and he who seeks finds, and to him who knocks it will be opened.* [9]*"Or what man is there among you who, when his son asks for a loaf, will give him a stone?* [10]*"Or if he asks for a fish, he will not give him a snake, will he?* [11]*"If you then, being evil, know how to give good gifts to your children, how much more will your Father who is in heaven give what is good to those who ask Him!)*

I do not make judgments on whether others have had failed attempts in the quest for things. I do not know what their fellowship with the father is like. I cannot even judge my future requests by all of my past failures, unless I judge what I asked for, how I asked for it, and why.

When we know who we are, then failure is not an option. Satan also points us to the failures of others to receive their desired answers from God. He points us to delays in answers to our prayers and the prayers of others. He says, "You see, that is why you should give up on this prayer gibberish. God does not really care about you or your situation."

A few words of wisdom will be helpful as you pray:
    (1) Know who and whose you are.
    (2) When the manifestations of your answers are slow, remember that delay does not mean cancelled.
    (3) You have the ability within you to speed up delivery by elongating your expectation confessions called gratitude, to an all day affair. In the book of James chapter 4 and verse 2 and 3 we read about prayer failure. It suggests that prayer failure is caused by two things:
    (a) Not asking
    (b) Asking with the wrong purpose, motives, or intentions when you receive. When we pray we are seeking to line our will up with the will of the father for his glory.

(James 4:2-3- [2]You want something but don't get it. You kill and covet, but you cannot have what you want. You quarrel and fight. You do not have, because you do not ask God. [3]When you ask, you do not receive, because you ask with wrong motives, that you may spend what you get on your pleasures.)

    My maturity level is critical to my receiving. As you read Galatians 3 and 4 you find that the blessings of Abraham are for every believer. However, if the believer is immature then they cannot receive fully. Mature children of God do not have to fear at all. They never fear the response of their father. The question is not if, but when. And the when is often determined by our faith or faithfulness, which is evidenced by our confessions (good or bad). What is fear anyway? When I know whose I am, I do not have to fear. I am a child of God from the seed of Abraham. I have a right to be blessed and I am growing daily to ready myself for my inheritance.

Fatigue

"I am too tired. Prayer (and study) takes too much time and effort." Let me ask you a question. If you knew that getting up an hour earlier everyday would better your health, would you do it? If you knew that getting up an hour earlier everyday would bless your marriage would you do it? If you knew that getting up an hour earlier everyday would sharpen your thinking, would you do it? What about change your attitude, give you strength, build your confidence, lengthen your life, and teach you how to use your money properly, would you do it? Of course you would. Prayer doesn't cause fatigue. You are not too tired to pray. You are not too busy to pray. You and I have been fooled into believing that it is too time-consuming and tiring. I contend that it is our source of fuel for every other thing on our agenda. It helps us achieve those things with maximum effectiveness. It causes us to use the wisdom of God with all we do.

Pressure

Someone once said that pressure is the element by which character is made out of, that a person can see their real makeup based upon how they respond to pressure. The Oxford Universal Dictionary defines pressure as "the condition of being painfully oppressed in body or mind: affliction oppression: the action of anything that influences the mind or will, or a constraining influence."[4] Funk and Wagnall's Standard Dictionary adds' "the urgent demands on ones time and strength."[5]

Pressure comes as a result of many things: poor planning, an overload of job requests, peer success or influence; spousal tension; financial challenges. Any of the above can influence the mind or body to tense up and act abnormally. Some people feel that they do their best work under pressure. Athletes like to believe this especially. It is a sign of greatness. When the game is on the line I can perform at my peak. That is great, but a life is not made to be lived daily, constantly under pressure. God has equipped us with something called "adrenaline" for intense situations, but life itself was not planned with this as a normal function.

Pressure for most people spells panic. Panic means to find unusual means to solve problems. Often that invites trouble to come. Pressure in most peoples' life is an open door for enemy invasion. The disciples were under pressure and they went and hid out. Peter went back to his comfort zone, fishing. For others, that could be drinking, smoking, old friends, illegal trading of goods and services (the streets call it hustling).

John Koenig writes, "As always, the life story of Jesus shows that he understands the worst of our depths, because he has been there Himself. When He cried out from the cross, "My God, my God, why have you forsaken me?" he felt an emptiness that we can scarcely begin to comprehend. According to the Gospel writers, His relationship with his Abba (daddy) was more intimate, more trusting than that of any human being. But then as he came to a horrible end, the God who had sent him on his mission was no where to be found."

Pressure causes parental abuse, spousal abuse, marital separation, and even suicide to name a few. There is but one-way to close the door when pressure surfaces. Go into "warfare prayer mode." The greater the pressure the more time you need with God. Do not allow the enemy to trap you into believing any situation is too hard for God to handle. If he can raise a dead son, he can handle your situation. He has seen it all before. Your case is not a burden for Him. He lives to help you. Ask Him now.

Koenig goes on to deal with what Jesus was experiencing which was absolute loneliness or desolation which comes from the Latin word which means to abandon or forsake someone. It is here where we see pressure. "Clearly the term desolation is meant to apply to a wide range of mental and bodily status (depression, grief, pain, nausea, rage, shame, weakness). What they have in common, however, is the definite sensation that no one – especially God – seems ready or able to receive us from our peril." We sometimes feel so pressured that we think death is upon us and whatever character flaws or defects we have are heightened or surface when we are under pressure.

Well, now that we have some understanding of the enemies' traps, it is time to ward him off at the path. Are you ready to ambush him? Then let us walk through the next phase and learn the rules for engaging the heavens and arming ourselves with power that releases victory wherever our feet trod.

Chapter 5

"The Rules of Engagement"

II Chronicles 7:12:24: [12] *the LORD appeared to him at night and said: "I have heard your prayer and have chosen this place for myself as a temple for sacrifices.* [13] *"When I shut up the heavens so that there is no rain, or command locusts to devour the land or send a plague among my people,* [14] *if my people, who are called by my name, will humble themselves and pray and seek my face and turn from their wicked ways, then will I hear from heaven and will forgive their sin and will heal their land.*

    A rule is a prescribed method or procedure by which one follows in order to achieve a desired goal. In this case to have success in our prayer lives, there are principles or rules that need to be applied so that we have an encounter with God. Many people live their whole Christian lives unfulfilled because they do not have a clue how to enter into the presence of God. Over the next two chapters we will deal with the rules of engagement and the tools for engagement, then, we will be able to "Enter into His Presence."

    There are at least two principle rules of engagement that scripture affirms when it comes to prayer: (1) We must ask, and (2) We must ask correctly. The entire Bible has some form of prayer life included in it. Prayer in its simplest form is communication with God. It involves adoration, confessions, thanksgiving, and supplication, as well as intercession, which is another model we will investigate in a later writing, but is inclusive as well, in the model we will offer in chapters six through nine. The closing chapter will offer a small preview of intercessory prayer and what we will endeavor to share in a later writing. But now, let us take a look at these rules.

Rule One: Asking

II Chronicles 1: 7; That night God appeared to Solomon and said to him, "Ask for whatever you want me to give you."

Matthew 7: 7-11; [7]"Ask and it will be given to you; seek and you will find; knock and the door will be opened to you. [8]For everyone who asks receives; he who seeks finds; and to him who knocks, the door will be opened. [9]"Which of you, if his son asks for bread, will give him a stone? [10]Or if he asks for a fish, will give him a snake? [11]If you, then, though you are evil, know how to give good gifts to your children, how much more will your Father in heaven give good gifts to those who ask him!

James 4: 1-3; [1]What causes fights and quarrels among you? Don't they come from your desires that battle within you? [2]You want something but don't get it. You kill and covet, but you cannot have what you want. You quarrel and fight. You do not have, because you do not ask God. [3]When you ask, you do not receive, because you ask with wrong motives, that you may spend what you get on your pleasures.

In prayer, the asking part is really a posture of submission. It is an understanding that we are creatures of need. We have an inability to function properly without the guidance of our creator. It is His spirit in us that gives us life, purpose, and meaning.

The three scriptures above intimate that a relationship is the key to receiving from God in fullness. Solomon was in the inheritance bloodline and God said to him ask whatever you want and it's yours. Jesus, teaching the disciples, says to them in essence, you are connected to me. My dad is your dad. He loves you. Ask for what you want and you can get it. The writing of James says, "The reason you do not have what you desire is because you have not asked your father yet." While more is added to this, it is the first stage to engagement. You cannot experience the treasures of a relationship with God without communication. He encourages us to ask him something. Saul asked Jesus, on the road to Damascus "Who are you Lord?" It began a long and fruitful relationship with Jesus (even though it was a slow, lonely beginning as He tried to enter fellowship with the disciples). This is an important lesson to learn. Do not allow your relationship with people to affect your relationship with God. Allow your relationship with God to affect a change in you, and it will in turn affect the people you are in or seek to be with in relationship.

Those of us who have children will all admit that hearing the voice of our children say, "Daddy, could you buy me this?" is often a heart pause. If we are able to provide the request and we determine that it adds worth, value or an approved pleasure, then we make it happen. That same request can come from a stranger's child in a grocery basket or department store and be ignored, grinned upon, refused, or maybe even agreed to because of pity. The differences in the responses are solely dependent upon the relationship.

In Ephesians Chapter 3, Paul shares with the church how he came to have his insight, wisdom, and revelation of God and for what purpose. He says in verse 7 and 8 (KJV) *"[7]Whereof I was made a minister, according to the gift of the grace of God given unto me by the effectual working of his power. [8]Unto me, who am less than the least of all saints, is this grace given that I should preach among the Gentiles the unsearchable riches of Christ;"* indicating that he saw himself as a late bloomer in the Kingdom of God, but nonetheless a significant part of the family. You should make that confession over your life daily. "I am a small but important part of the family of God. I have a purpose. I am fulfilling my purpose daily. My father helps me do that."

Paul comes to verse 12 of that same chapter and gives to the church a posture of prayer before he begins to actually pray for them (or express what he prays for them). He says, *"In whom we have boldness and access with confidence by the faith of him..."* Paul is helping us to understand that the relationship that we have with Jesus, our fellowship with him, and believing that he can perform any task, allows us to approach the Father without fear of rejection. The Hebrew writer speaks again and again about the relationship with Jesus as well. It speaks in two places, Hebrews 4: 14-16 and Hebrews 10: 14-23 of our right to come boldly to the throne of God because of our relationship to Jesus and his blood. The suggestion is that when the Father sees us covered by the blood of Jesus he does not see us as sinners, but as sons and daughters and therefore must hear our requests with joy and preparation for delivery.

WHY ASK?

Have you often wondered why does God require asking if He is all knowing? I have as well. First of all, children do not know everything. They often desire things that are not good for them and if they do not ask they do not know why's and how's. Secondly, asking keeps the child in the state of understanding the relationship. I am a child, He is my father, and I need Him to navigate through this life. His counsel, wisdom, knowledge, and understanding are where I receive mine from, and in order for mine to grow we need to communicate. Asking questions opens up a dialogue. I then learn how my father thinks so I can think like him.

Thirdly, asking reminds me of the source of everything that I have. I may know my parent has my allowance every week, but I should never go in their pockets or in their dresser drawers to take it. It is mine, it is promised and therefore I have it, but I either wait for their time to give it to me because they know the right time for distribution, or I request it, ask for it, when I think I need it and wait for their decision on whether they see what I see. Asking helps me to stay appreciative of my source. If I do not have to ask, then I may forget to appreciate the location of my blessings.

Rule Two: Asking Correctly

James 4:3 When you ask, you do not receive, because you ask with wrong motives, that you may spend what you get on your pleasures.

James 4:10; humble yourselves before the Lord and he will lift you up

There are at least six ways that we find in scriptures that help us achieve an audience with the Father. It is not just asking, but how we ask that matters. When we ask correctly we open up the floodgate of opportunity for blessings. The power works inside of us and draws from the gates of heaven, 'the realm of overflow'.

Matthew 6: 5-8; [5]*"And when you pray, do not be like the hypocrites, for they love to pray standing in the synagogues and on the street corners to be seen by men. I tell you the truth; they have received their reward in full.* [6]*But when you pray, go into your room, close the door and pray to your Father, who is unseen. Then you're Father, who sees what is done in secret, will reward you.* [7]*And when you pray, do not keep on babbling like pagans, for they think they will be heard because of their many words.* [8]*Do not be like them, for your Father knows what you need before you ask him.*

Eph 3: 17-20; [17]*so that Christ may dwell in your hearts through faith. And I pray that you, being rooted and established in love,* [18]*may have power, together with all the saints, to grasp how wide and long and high and deep is the love of Christ,* [19]*and to know this love that surpasses knowledge—that you may be filled to the measure of all the fullness of God.* [20]*Now to him who is able to do immeasurably more than all we ask or imagine, according to his power that is at work within us,*

Have you ever had someone come to ask you for something and they said, "Give me five dollars or a ride to the store," as if you owed it to them? Sometimes the person asking does not even know you. Other times the person in question is in relationship with you, but the way they asked you was not in the right spirit or you think that their motive was to use the money or ride to do something that would be detrimental to them or to you. There are certain attitudes and asking that do not move heaven to respond in favor of our requests. It is therefore important to gain knowledge and understanding of how to get our prayers answered without enemy interference. If you will use these rules for asking you will begin to see answered prayer on a consistent basis, not just a hit and miss experience. Our Father wants us living a fulfilled life, a life more abundant. When we pray right we can do that. Then we move into the place where we begin to experience the "Altared Life".

Boldness

Hebrews 4:14-16 (KJV) ¹⁴Seeing then those we have a great high priest that is passed into the heavens, Jesus the Son of God; let us hold fast our profession.
¹⁵For we have not a high priest, which cannot be touched with the feeling of our infirmities; but was in all points tempted like as we are, yet without sin.
¹⁶Let us therefore come boldly unto the throne of grace that we may obtain mercy, and find grace to help in time of need.

I heard a story about a pastor who was in the pulpit preparing the preaching event. The church was full to capacity upstairs in the sanctuary and downstairs in the overflow. They were not letting anyone else into the building. A young boy came to the door and the ushers told him that they could not let him in because of the crowd being too large. They apologized and asked the boy to come another time. The boy looked in the eyes of the doorkeeper and responded by saying, "Sir, do you see that man in the pulpit, well that's my daddy, and I know he wants me to come in to be with him. There is a space for me down front somewhere, just you go and see. Ask my dad."

Our relationship with Jesus allows us to enter into the presence of God without fear of rejection or unworthiness. His blood over our lives has covered our sinful past, present and future. It causes the Father's eyes to see Christ when he looks at us. The Son in us is the image of God, as the Hebrew writer declares "…the exact representation of his being" (Hebrews 1:3 NIV).

When you develop an intimate relationship with the Lord, you know you can call and ask anything of Him. No conversation is too long. No question is too far out. He is dad. He longs to help us. Therefore He desires us to come and talk to Him about any and everything.

When I am in my prayer room at home, I have the outer door closed and it has an inner sliding door I keep closed as well. If my son wants me, and my wife turns her back to do something, he will find me. He will open both doors and boldly stand there with a big grin on his face saying, "Daddy, what are you doing?" He has no shame, no doubts, no fears, and no apprehension. He knows his daddy will see him. As busy as daddy might be, he will pause to acknowledge and address the requests of his son. Our heavenly Father has an open door policy with his children. No matter how busy he may be with all he has to oversee in the world, He is never too busy for you and me. What a dad!

Humility

James 4:4-10
[4]You adulterous people, don't you know that friendship with the world is hatred toward God? Anyone who chooses to be a friend of the world becomes an enemy of God. [5]Or do you think Scripture says without reason that the spirit he caused to live in us envies intensely? [6]But he gives us more grace. That is why Scripture says:
 "God opposes the proud but gives grace to the humble.
[7]Submit yourselves, then, to God. Resist the devil, and he will flee from you. [8]Come near to God and he will come near to you. Wash your hands, you sinners, and purify your hearts, you double-minded. [9] Grieve, mourn and wail. Change your laughter to mourning and your joy to gloom. [10]Humble yourselves before the Lord and he will lift you up.

Humility is a quality or characteristic ascribed to a person who is considered to be humble. A humble person is generally thought to be unpretentious and modest: someone who does not think that he or she is better or more important than others.

It appears contradictory, to in one breath talk about coming to God in boldness, then in another breath talk about coming to God in humility. Yet, boldness is the approach because of the relationship and humility is the posture that speaks of the nature of the relationship. Bold because we are related, humble because of how we are related. The nature of our relationship is one of father and child, provider and recipient, giver and receiver. This is one reason for approaching in humility. I recognize the awesome ability of my Father. I reverence, respect his authority, and his wisdom to guide me. I am grateful for him adopting me into his family although I was an unworthy child, because I did not recognize my created worth. Therefore, I lived unrestrained, visionless and allowed Satan to trick me into believing his rewards were all I needed.

Another reason for humility in our approaching the presence of God is because there are times when areas of your life have experienced failure. You have failed in your love walk. Your tongue has written things in your life that were contrary to biblical confessions. You have done things that were not done by faith, therefore it was sin (*Romans 13:2-3, ²Consequently, he who rebels against the authority is rebelling against what God has instituted, and those who do so will bring judgment on themselves. ³For rulers hold no terror for those who do right, but for those who do wrong. Do you want to be free from fear of the one in authority? Then do what is right and he will commend you.*). Whatever we do great or small that is a fall back into the life of "the old man," flesh, needs repentance. Repentance is a turning away from the act, attitude, and ambition, to do or be involved in ungodly behavior and turn towards God. When we turn towards God, we turn towards Prayer, the Word, Godly counsel (pastors, teachers, prophets, evangelists, apostles, deacons, who meet biblical standards).

Humility in this sense is an attitude of sorrow for sin with the understanding that even though my relationship is intact I have broken fellowship with God. I come boldly because he is still my dad, but I come in humility because I have dishonored Him. I have not worn or carried the family name well and I have come to apologize, ask for forgiveness, and seek counsel about correction and restoration. Proverbs 15:3, *"The fear of the LORD teaches man wisdom, and humility comes before honor."*

My actions make me undeserving of "sonship" privileges. He is so loving; however, that he will hear me and restore me because of His name in me (His Son) as I draw nearer to him. I draw nearer by submitting to his authority, His word over my life. I agree to abide by the principles He has set up for me to live by, and reject the ones the world has to offer. I declare, "You know more about life and living than I do, and I yield to your instruction. Help me to do it your way." Then I remove myself from the "ear hearing" of the enemy. This may mean the end of some relationships I thought I desperately needed. As the words of one song says,

All I need is you Lord, Is you Lord, All I need is you...

How true that song is, when all is said and done, when you get down to how we are able to handle the rest of our life with care, He is all we need. Humble yourself and access his presence once again. A fall is not failure unless you failed to fall back in love with Him. You are always merely "humility" away, from His feet. If you can get to his feet, you can touch the "hem of his garment. If you can touch the hem of his garment you can experience his hands. If you can experience his hands, you will not be satisfied until you behold His face.

In Faith

Merriam- Webster's dictionary defines faith as, "belief and trust in and loyalty to God; firm belief in something for which there is no proof; or complete trust." Hebrews 11:1 says this about faith, "now faith is being sure of what we hope for and certain of what we do not see." Understanding faith and applying it is critical to answered prayer as well as living a life that is pleasing to God.

Mike Flynn in his book The Mustard Seed Book, shares that the bible gives us four kinds of faith. If you desire to live and benefit from the Christian life it is essential that you grasp this foundational understanding.

The first is *the faith*. *The faith* is what Christians believe and will defend as the truth. The truth of who God is. *Hebrews 11:6, and without faith it is impossible to please God, because anyone who comes to him must believe that he exists and that he rewards those who earnestly seek him.* This is the Christian faith as a whole. The belief, that it is the answer, for a lost world. It is the only hope to return a fallen humanity to its creator, a loving God.

The second is *saving faith,* which is the ability God gives people to believe in Jesus as Savior, forgiver and Lord. It is saving faith to say; "Jesus is Lord". It is acknowledging what God has done. You need saving faith to establish the relationship. "I believe he died for my sins". I believe the Father raised Him from the dead. I believe He lives in me to lead me and guide me in all things.

The third kind is the *gift of faith*, which is a sort of booster shot by which we lay hold of grace that is beyond our normal grasp. It is believing in what God will do; believing in miracles. It is a strong, unyielding confidence in everything God says and the boldness to declare it to others, convincing them to see beyond the not yet seen. [8]

The fourth kind is the business of *having faith*, or *normal faith*, which is concerned with a personal day-to day- relationship with God and the world or what God is doing right now. Romans 8:28 is a perfect example of this. It is the belief that everything will work out for my good because I am in a covenant relationship with God.

You need faith. Faith coupled with love is a non-negotiable. Life does not work without it. Everybody has it. We use it everyday. We trust meteorologists (weather people), cars, traffic lights, bridges, elevators etc., what about the creator of the universe?

Mark 11:24- Therefore I tell you, whatever you ask for in prayer, believe that you have received it, and it will be yours.

What a marvelous discovery this is for the believer. We can have what we desire and say, if we believe that the Father will give it to us. Our faith and our words are therefore very powerful tools. We will discuss that further in the next chapter.

It is important for us to have a consistency with the scriptures. When Jesus said this, he was speaking to his disciples. It was with the understanding that these men had His heart or were developing His heart for the Father's will to be done in the earth. Therefore they would not pray according to fleshly desires.

Psalm 37:4-5: [4] *Delight yourself in the LORD and he will give you the desires of your heart.* [5] *Commit your way to the LORD; trust in him and he will do this:*

I John 5:14-15: [14]*This is the confidence we have in approaching God: that if we ask anything according to his will, he hears us.* [15]*And if we know that he hears us—whatever we ask—we know that we have what we asked of him.*

Prayer has a catch to it. It must be done "<u>in faith</u>" and according to "<u>the faith</u>". Delighting myself in the Lord is a prerequisite to petition hearing. Pleasing Him means to live by faith, trusting that His Word is the guiding voice in all my affairs. If I delight myself in this, I can have the desires of my heart. The simple truth is this, my heart and His are mirror images. My will is His will, and His will is mine. I am now his ambassador in the earth. I do what He says and say what He says and He gives me what I need to do it.

Before you begin to pray, especially when you are praying for healing or deliverance, you should search the scriptures or recite them (say them aloud) so that you and your hearers can gain faith for what is to occur. The gospels are full of stories about healing and deliverance. Here are several passages to read to increase your faith in God for miracles. The principles work if you work the principles.

For Healing
- James 5:15
- Luke 13:10-17
- Luke 17:11-19
- Acts 3:1-10

For Deliverance
- Mark 2:1-12
- Mark 5:1-20
- Mark 9:14-29

For Supernatural Occurrences
- 2 Kings 2
- James 5:17
- Joshua 10:8-14
- Mark 11: 12-25

Wisdom

James 1: 5-8; ⁵If any of you lacks wisdom, he should ask God, who gives generously to all without finding fault, and it will be given to him. ⁶But when he asks, he must believe and not doubt, because he who doubts is like a wave of the sea, blown and tossed by the wind.

⁷That man should not think he will receive anything from the Lord; ⁸he is a double-minded man, unstable in all he does.

Webster defines wisdom as "the quality or state of being wise; knowledge of what is true or right, coupled with just judgment as to action; prudence, discernment, or insight."

The Word of God teaches us that we have a Father who is full of wisdom and awaits an opportunity to download it into His children. It is as simple as asking. Not just one time though, but for every situation that arises we should desire wisdom so that we make God honoring decisions.

In the first chapter of the letter of James, it begins by talking about how to handle trials and temptations with patience, believing that the end will result in victory. In order to endure these trials one must have patience. In order to acquire patience, prayer is needed. The focus of prayer in the midst of trials must be on a request for wisdom. "Father, help me to see trials like you see them, to say what you say through them, and use the lessons that lead to victory in the present storm to encourage me in the next one." Each trail then becomes a lesson. Every new lesson is seen as a stepping stone to new benefits, blessings and stewardship responsibilities in the Kingdom of God.

The book of Proverbs is a gold mine of information that develops and encourages the believer in the area of wisdom. You should read a chapter everyday for the rest of your life. Before you go further, take a moment to read the following to get the importance of wisdom:

Proverbs 1: 1-7 (If you don't have a Bible, see Appendix A)
Proverbs 2
Proverbs 3
Proverbs 4: 5-12 (See Appendix A)

If you do not have a bible with you read, it later. But read it. Hey, I'm serious. READ IT! PLEASE! When you read these chapters you see how important a relationship with God is. Consequently you see how important prayer is. Wisdom is what you use in your everyday life to glorify God. It is the God way of thinking. It is Word based and prayer inspired thinking. I ask God for ideas according to His will for the earth. I use His revelation to bless Him. In the process, He blesses me. He pours into my life the bible meaning of prosperity. It is not merely money talk, it is image talk that leads to 'shalom', peace that passes understanding. It is the understanding that I have full benefits as a child of God. My needs are met if my name is changed. He delights in me experiencing heaven on earth. Read this insight for more insight:

Proverbs 3:21-26; [21] My son, preserve sound judgment and discernment, do not let them out of your sight; [22] they will be life for you, an ornament to grace your neck. [23] Then you will go on your way in safety, and your foot will not stumble; [24] when you lie down, you will not be afraid; when you lie down, your sleep will be sweet. [25] Have no fear of sudden disaster or of the ruin that overtakes the wicked, [26] for the LORD will be your confidence and will keep your foot from being snared.

Proverbs 3:33-35: [33] The Lord's curse is on the house of the wicked, but he blesses the home of the righteous. [34] He mocks proud mockers but gives grace to the humble. [35] The wise inherit honor, but fools he holds up to shame.

When I use wisdom, His will, and words in my life as a practice, as a habit rather than a hobby, then I can expect certain things to happen in my life. Does this mean no crosses to bear? Well, no. The cross for my salvation, He bore that. But I will have to bear the burden of whatever work I am called to. The good news is that I have grace for my assignments. The blessing of the Lord makes me rich, nothing missing, and nothing broken, gives me peace, and adds no sorrow. I am not devastated by the approach of problems. I have the answer inside of me. That answer is the anointing of God. I describe the anointing as the power of God, to destroy yokes and remove burdens from ones life, so that they can achieve their divine destiny. All of us have an assignment. Yokes and burdens, sin, distractions, vices, illegitimate relationships, love of money, rebellion on the job, at home, in church, financial debts, marital division, parental inability etc., will slow your arrival (if not prevent it) to where God has planned for you to be. Do not die in the desert when the Promised Land is so close. Wisdom is described in I Corinthians 1: 30 as the anointing that is in Jesus. The power, the Word, and the mind of Jesus are the wisdom of

God. His word is wisdom. His word is power. His word produces righteousness, holiness and redemption. Therefore, pray the Word. Now *that* is wisdom. As time goes on you will be so filled with Him that you will receive the full revelation of who you are. You are '*a*' Word from God.

If you pray the Word, you cannot pray "amiss" (*James 1:6 But when he asks, he must believe and not doubt, because he who doubts is like a wave of the sea, blown and tossed by the wind.*) You will have:

(1) The right nature/mindset
    a. I do not do this for vain glory
    b. I am a Kingdom representative (ambassador). I am He in the earth. His words are my words and mine are His.

(2) The right make up
    a. I know sin can't be present in my life, and answers flow consistently.
    b. I practice holiness and revelation knowledge is available to me.

In the Name

John 14:14; you may ask me for anything in my name and I will do it.

John 16:23b... I tell you the truth, my Father will give you whatever you ask in my name.

All of us have heard the age old saying, "It's not what you know; it's who you know". Well, I disagree. I believe they both matter. Sometimes it is *'what'* you know about the *'whom'* you know, that really matters. There are some things you cannot get accomplished in life without knowing someone with enough clout to get you into the places you need to be. You must know influential people in life if you are ever to succeed. As a matter of fact everyone has influence somewhere. The key to life is finding the person or person's who have influence in the places you need them. If you want to engage the Father, you need to know Jesus and use his name when you speak to Him. Its not just about the name, however, it's the relationship.

Listen to the model prayer and you hear Jesus teaching us to pray to the Father. He mentions it again in one of the passages above (John 16), but He adds this, "in my name". The Father answers to requests in Jesus' name. When petitions, supplications are made in the name of Jesus they give indication to the Father that he is hearing from an adopted child. Jesus who the bible says, intercedes for us at the right hand of the Father, confirms, "Yes, I know them," so the Father grants the request.

It is significant to note that the name is not the pass alone. It is the spirit of the name. It is the relationship associated with the name. Is the name in the person using it or are they carrying someone else's identification card? You can be arrested for driving on someone else's license. In the book of Acts, chapter 19, there is a story about the seven sons of Sceva. They tried to use the name of Jesus to cast out evil spirits as they had seen Paul the Apostle do, but the evil spirit said to them, "Jesus I know, Paul I know, but who you are?"(v.15) Then the spirits commenced to attack them with such violence that seven men ran off naked, exposed for being impostors. Heaven and hell know and respect that name, but it cannot be someone else's license. You have a license to use it. When you do, it will get you results from the Father.

One other note that few talk about; There are times when we can talk to Jesus directly and ask Him in his name to do things for us. John 14:14 indicates this to us. Jesus says, ask me and if I know you, then I will serve you. That is powerful. Our elder brother is at our service to do what we need Him to do. Is He not the greatest brother ever? My heart yearns to be that kind of brother to my siblings (natural and spiritual).

Without Ceasing

Luke 18:1 (MSG) Jesus told them a story showing that it was necessary for them to pray consistently and never quit.

I Thessalonians 5:16-18 (MSG) Be cheerful no matter what; pray all the time; thank God no matter what happens. This is the way God wants you who belong to Christ Jesus to live.

Matthew 7:7; Ask and it will be given to you; seek and you will find; knock and the door will be opened to you.

One of the strangest requests in the bible has to be this one. When the bible tells us to pray without ceasing, is God assuming that we have nothing else to do? On the contrary; He knows that we have much to do and to do it without a life that's saturated with prayer is to experience misguidance and failure on a consistent basis. The kind of prayer God desires from us is one of unbroken fellowship. There are no moments that we are un-open to hear His voice or speak to Him. We often see prayer as us talking, but what about the hearing aspect? Does not our Father speak to us in prayer? Therefore, if I am in prayer daily (especially first thing in the morning), then when faced with any issue, I seek His advice, are not my ears open to hear His answer? If that be the case, then I am in the constant state of prayer. If we believe that, we cannot gossip, slander, participate in unnatural sexual behavior, lie steal, cheat, become intoxicated etc., because we will bring undesired static into the communication lines and be unable to clearly hear our directions. No wonder many churchgoers are miserable in this Christian walk.

It is interesting to note that in the gospel of Matthew, Jesus tells us just before he teaches us the "Model Prayer", not to use "vain repetitions (KJV)" when we pray. He says the Father knows what we need when we pray anyway. So then why are we praying? For one, because he said so! Right after He says the Father knows before you ask, He says, "This is how you should pray…" suggesting that prayer should happen and also that it should have order or structure. It should address key areas: God as Father; Us as Kingdom preparers; Request for spiritual substance (word); Direction; Deliverance; Forgiveness and Forgiving of others.

In chapter 7 of Matthew we see what I heard one man of God call in my early years of ministry, "the ascending power of prayer." The first phase is the asking stage where our requests are made to God. The second stage is our seeking stage, which addresses our faith in what we asked for. The final state is knocking which is the stage of perseverance or persistence added to faith.

While the asking stage is the stage for beginners, I believe if the seeking stage is the one of faith then it is the stage of confessing the word and believing that our angels are working to bring our confessions to pass. The bible teaches us that angels have assignments. One of the assignments is to hearken to the crics of Christ. *(Matthew 26:53 KJV; Thinkest thou that I cannot now pray to my Father and he shall presently give me more than twelve legions of angels?)* Now if Christ is in me, then when I speak, their assignment is to take my words and bring them to pass. Do yourself a favor and do a study on Angels. Begin with Hebrews 1:7-14 and Psalm 90, so you can see that you have help that you cannot always see.

I believe the seeking stage is the stage that also involves inquiry of the Father. It asks questions like, "Where do you want me to go so that I am in position to receive my requests?" It seeks His will daily so that we are not out of position when the answer manifests itself.

The knocking state is the stage where we bombard heaven with praise for the expected results.

1. If I ask for a job, I am specific about my request. I ask for a place. I ask for a salary. I ask for work times I desire that enhance my spiritual life and my family life.
2. I fill out the application where I want to go. I confess my success. I then clean up anything in my life that hinders my ability to move quickly to manifestation or that displeases my Father and may cause promise delay. I daily seek his face for direction and protection.
3. I make my confessions of thanksgiving daily and often and I fully expect a breakthrough.

When I was in college at Illinois State University, I needed a job to help me with my undisciplined social life. I filled out an application at a grocery store that had no people of color working there. They told me "Thanks, we will call you". One week later I returned and inquired about a job. They said, "No, we are not hiring, we will call you though. Do not call us". Another week went by and I returned. This time they told me, "Sir, please don't come back, you can have the job, and you start in two weeks". I received the job because of the knocking stage. I expected it and wouldn't take no for an answer. I believed that no matter what the circumstances were, I was going to get a job there and I would not quit showing up until I did. Can God depend on you having that posture in prayer or worship or study? He finds favor with the faithful; the crowd that will not cease. Are you one of them? If not, change your position today and begin experiencing his awesome presence and presents daily and often.

Chapter 6

"The Tools for Engagement"

II Peter 1:3 His divine power has given us everything we need for life and godliness through our knowledge of him who called us by his own glory and goodness.

    What would you think of a surgeon who came to the operating room to perform surgery, but came late and showed up without their operating tools? Or an attorney who showed up late for court without his or her briefs? Of course you would think he or she was irresponsible, negligent, incompetent or at least inconsiderate of your desires to be healed or helped.
    We have a contractor that does our lawn. One week the caretaker showed up and I was looking for the lawn to be cut. He informed me that he didn't have his tools. His truck was in the shop. I wanted to know how my grass was going to get cut and why did he come if he couldn't do anything while he was there. The Christian life is such a powerful one, but it requires us to have certain tools for us to do our job properly. If we will bring certain tools to the prayer closet we can experience surging on our lives that will produce power. If we bring our tools to the prayer closet we will come out of it ready to experience life more abundantly. The "altared" life is the expected end of this journey. The "altared" life is the life I seek after. Again, it is the life lived constantly in the presence of God. My every awakened desire is communion with Him. That communion helps set the right attitude for every relationship and position I have in life.
    There are actually three parts to this chapter: (1) Understanding the Enemies Distractions; (2) Putting Your Self in

Position to Receive; and (3) Using the weapons that destroy the Enemy and Ensure Your Entrance into His Presence.

Understanding the Enemies Distractions

In the area of distraction it is important to note how Satan tries to use things near and dear to us to divert our attention. He does this so that we cannot find the time to pray or experience the power of God. We are distracted either by thinking about something we have to do or have done already.

Dr. Henry Malone writes, "Satan always attacks everything that will affect the outcome of God's purpose for our lives. Have you ever noticed how Satan tries to interrupt your life by causing disturbances or unnecessary conflicts? He is a master at interruptions and distractions. His intrusions can cause you to miss much of what God really intends for your life."

How right Dr. Malone is when he intimates that we were born to have unbroken fellowship with God and that we must be careful to keep watch of Satan who tries to interrupt that fellowship, so we lose focus of our assignments, because we are caught up in focusing on our circumstances.

Satan is a master at disguise. He will sometimes seek to convince us that we are so busy with ministry that we do not have time to pray. It is perfectly fine to read your bible because you may need to do a little of that to prepare a bible study or sermon for a meeting. On the other hand, if he can get you to borrow someone else's scriptures, message, or lesson, why study the bible, just the lesson. Satan discourages you from praying. You really do not need to waste your time in praying. You could be doing something really important like spending time with your wife, husband or children, which you have neglected this whole week. How about doing something for yourself like going shopping, playing golf, tennis, to a movie, riding your bike, entertaining some friends, washing that dirty car, or sleeping. You know you need to get a hobby. You work too much anyway.

All of those things I mentioned are significant to people. They come under the home, family and hobby category, which every person needs in their life in order to have a well-balanced and healthy life. However, if we eliminate prayer, we will participate in those areas, with those significant people, without the understanding of our true purpose in their lives. We also will fail to experience the love of God and therefore be clueless at expressing it to them in such a meaningful manner that it causes them to know Him intimately. When we are the manifested love of God in the lives of others, they get a glimpse of how life was truly meant to be lived. It is giving oneself unselfishly and unconditionally. You and I cannot do that alone without the help of our Father God.

When I am playing golf, sometimes I pray as I ride and walk; I use my hobby time to make my heart His home. I want God to know that I do not have any private time in my life where he is not welcome. He helps me have integrity in game playing, intimacy with my spouse, and patience with my children. You see, you really cannot ever be too busy to pray. If you are, then you are too busy.

Putting Yourself in the Position to Receive

There are a few tools of preparation that you need for your successful prayer time:

1. An appointment
2. An arena
3. An attitude
4. An atmosphere
5. An agenda

An Appointment

When talking about a meeting with God, it appears that you just have to stand in line and wait your turn to talk to him. This is not the kind of appointment to which I am referring. I am not suggesting that you make an appointment as though he is too busy to talk to you now. Rather make it a scheduled time to meet with him daily. Make it a point. Put it on your day planner as an appointment you cannot break, so that it becomes a routine engagement that impacts everyday of your life. The time of day really does matter, contrary to opinions. Why? Because early prayer before any enemy invasion, will keep you focused in the event of an attack. No wonder we read of David in the wilderness giving us instruction on how to overcome circumstances that appear out of ones control.

Psalm 63:1 O God, thou art my God; early will I seek thee: my soul thirsteth for thee, my flesh longeth for thee in a dry and thirsty land, where no water is; (KJV)

He first acknowledges God as Lord of creation, strong and mighty over all enemy forces. Then he clues us in on when to seek Him and how. I am aware as I pen these words that some who read are working different shifts, so that their nights are days and their days are nights. The concept however, does not change. Early signifies the first of your day. Give God the first of your day. Make an appointment with Him so that you can receive your orders for that day. Do it so that you can order your spirit man for the day. Do it so that your "flesh" does not take advantage of any opportunities to rise up and take charge. The voice you hear first and loudest in the morning (or your day), is significant to how you handle your assignments. Might I add this? An early appointed time will make you aware of the fact that your Father is available and anxious to hear you all day long about every matter that arises. The bible shares with us that our Lord modeled this as well. Jesus arose in the morning, to pray, according to Mark 1:35.

The Old Testament prophet, David, gives us an understanding of why he was such a powerful seer, and able to withstand captivity, while positioning himself to gain favor with the king so he could exercise his spiritual gifts and affect the nation.

Daniel 6:10 (NIV) offers us the example of the life of a man who took appointed times seriously. Daniel lived the altared life.

On his knees, three appointed times a day, was his answer to life's difficult moments. He faced trials on his knees. David writes in Psalm 55:17, *Evening, morning and noon I cry out in distress, and he hears my voice.* They had different circumstances; nevertheless they both saw the same solution. Appointed time with God was needed. Your life will never be the same when you make a decision to schedule the most important appointment you will ever have and keep it. So get out your calendar, your day timer, your computer, your blackberry, trio, Iphone or whatever new gadget is on the market as you are reading this, and schedule an appointment early tomorrow and every day thereafter, as many times as you can.

An Arena

Where is your prayer closet? Where is your altar? Where is the place you go to receive from God? Is there a room in your house that you have designated as the place where you pray? Do you have a special place in a park, by a tree, where you are alone with God? Abram built an altar to the Lord where God appeared and spoke to Him. Then moving to another place where he would take up resident, he built another altar where he called the name of the Lord. These are two different places, one where the Lord appeared to him (the worship place or church) and the other where you take up residence or where you call on Him in prayer (Genesis 12:6-9). In I Samuel 7 we find Samuel, the priest of the Lord, judging the children of Israel. He understands clearly that anyone in leadership of God's people (in a house of worship, on a job, in a home, in a social gathering or sporting event) needs to lead with integrity. In order to do that there must be consistency in fellowship with the Lord. To have this, an "altared" life is needed. Samuel was aware of this.

I Samuel 7:17 {NIV} says, *But he always went back to Ramah, where his home was, and there he also judged Israel. And he built an altar there to the LORD.*

Notice that the text says, "He always went back..." to the altar. We find our strength in the "altar-ed" life. It is the life that finds an arena to pray any and everywhere, until you become the arena. Jesus became an altar. People came near him and life change happened. Peter showed up and his shadow healed people. There are signs of an "altar-ed" life. It happens when you spend so much time in the arena where you pray that you look like, think like, act like, the Father. You have an image rebirth. You return to your original power and purpose. Dominion and fruitfulness are the order of your day and you multiply after the God kind.

The whole concept of the arena and the altar-ed life comes into focus in the scene called the "transfiguration." Notice one other passage of scripture before we get to the transfiguration passage in Luke 9. We want to establish that Jesus left the disciples to go off alone to a place to pray. Before you do corporate praying you should develop a private prayer life (unless you are a babe in Christ). If you are a babe in Christ then the reverse is so. Corporately pray, with heavenly intimate people, until you become intimate enough to meet on your own. It is important to note that there were times he took certain disciples with him as well, so they could see the worth of prayer for their lives as leaders of the world winning mission to which they had been called.

Luke 9: 28, 29 *[28]About eight days after Jesus said this, he took Peter, John and James with him and went up onto a mountain to pray. [29]As he was praying, the appearance of his face changed, and his clothes became as bright as a flash of lightning.*

It is ironic that Peter and John became two of the early leaders of the church. They were seers of the glory in Jesus while prayer took place. Obviously the mountain was a favorite prayer arena for Jesus, because we note that He was there when it was his hour to be sacrificed for the sins of the world (*Matthew 26: 42-46 [42]He went away a second time and prayed, "My Father, if it is not possible for this cup to be taken away unless I drink it, may your will be done." [43]When he came back, he again found them sleeping, because their eyes were heavy. [44]So he left them and went away once more and prayed the third time, saying the same thing. [45]Then he returned to the disciples and said to them, "Are you still sleeping and resting? Look, the hour is near, and the Son of Man is betrayed into the hands of sinners. [46]Rise, let us go! Here comes my betrayer!"*). Where is your arena, altar, favorite prayer place? Today is a great day to establish one.

An Atmosphere

When I was in high school, as well as my early days of college, I considered myself a lover of slow love songs, or what was called "doowaps." I am not sure where the word came from, but the music was absolutely enchanting. No party was right without them. We often played fast songs, 45's, LP's, Eight tracks,

Reel to reels, (I am dating myself) to set an excitement in the room. People danced together in lines and in twosomes, (bopping or "two stepping"). Sometimes the couples were two guys dancing together, or two girls dancing together, because they had practiced choreographed moves. It was like a dance contest. This was always great excitement. My crew often brought our favorite records (James Brown) so we could do special choreographed "bump" dancing. The lights were flashing (black lights or strobe lights, high or real low depending on the music played). Like clockwork, at the end of every party the music would slow down, the light dimmed, and everyone would seek out a partner who they really liked or desired intimacy with and slow danced until they sent us home. As I write now, I take a deep breath. What a time! I often bought my own slow records or went to the Disk Jockey and requested a favorite song, because I wanted to set the atmosphere for that close personal moment with the girl I was interested in (or dating at the time). The mood for the dance and "rap" (smooth talk in the ear of a member of the opposite sex, generally guy to girl) was important.

Have you ever wanted to impress someone? Or wanted to take your spouse out to dinner? Then you know that choosing or setting the right atmosphere is very important. The lights, the music, and the décor are all significant. Mark 1:35, which we read earlier, notes that Jesus went to a "solitary place" to pray. I want to make some atmosphere setting suggestions for you so that you are equipped to get the most out of your prayer time.

1. A Quiet Place: A place where you will not be distracted by phones, pagers, television, children. You must be able to hear what God is saying to you through his word, a song, or silence.

2. Strategic Music. Soft music sets the atmosphere to love on God. The music should be focused. If you are praying the temple prayer or the model prayer or the A.C.T.S. method, have music on to prompt your thanksgiving, praise and worship. Use an ipod, mp3 player, itunes, or boom box, CD player with planned selections if you can. They can be without words or with words. It should be soft enough to concentrate on praying, but loud enough to give you a phrase to prompt you to continue. Find music on the blood

of Jesus, the Lamb of God, healing, surrender, forgiveness, the Holy Spirit, and the praise of His name.

3. Pen and Paper: While you read the Word of God and you are meditating on something you read or just listening for a response to something you just said, it is good to have a pen and paper ready to write. You may receive one word or one book. Write it and begin working on it. Many of my songs and book outlines come in the hour of prayer. When the atmosphere is right you can hear God say anything.

4. Other tools you might use to set the atmosphere are: incense candles, a talitt (prayer shield) used in the Jewish cultures, worn as a covering around the neck.

An Attitude

Attitude in prayer is as significant as it is in every area of life. I met a group of girls in an airport heading to a cheerleading competition. I asked them who was going to win. One of them shrugged her shoulders and said, "I don't know." The truth was, she was right, but the answer I was looking for from her was not about the reality of the outcome of the event, but their mental preparation.

I have always been intrigued by the mentality of great athletes. Muhammad Ali's, Michael Jordan's, Bill Russell, Larry Bird, Roger Clemons, Bob Gibson, Jimmy Connors, Jack Nicklaus and Tiger Woods, all of which believed when they stepped out on their respective fields, courts, or course of play, that they would be victorious. They expected to win.

Whenever we approach the throne room of God, we should go with expectation. You should never go into your prayer time with the attitude that this is a mere routine visit or useless chatter. Go expecting to hear and experience something life changing. Go listening for a shift in every adverse wind that blows in your life. Go listening for a Word to share with your spouse, children, siblings, co-workers, boss, neighbor, the store clerk, your friends, and your enemies. Go looking for and expecting an assignment. Whose life can you help change today and how? Then, get excited about your encounter. Don't you know that the father is excited to hear from you? If you knew what you were in store for you would be excited to see him as well. It is Christmas morning every morning. Our daddy has been planning something special for us and he cannot wait for us to approach Him to receive it. Note this prayer of expectation and excitement found in the book of Acts:

Acts 4:23-31 On their release, Peter and John went back to their own people and reported all that the chief priests and elders had said to them. ^{24}When they heard this, they raised their voices together in prayer to God. "Sovereign Lord," they said, "you made the heaven and the earth and the sea, and everything in them. ^{25}You spoke by the Holy Spirit through the mouth of your servant, our father David:" 'Why do the nations rage and the peoples plot in vain? ^{26}The kings of the earth take their stand and the rulers gather together against the Lord and against his Anointed One.' ^{27}Indeed Herod and Pontius Pilate met together with the Gentiles and the people of Israel in this city to conspire against your holy servant Jesus, whom you anointed. ^{28}They did what your power and will had decided beforehand should happen. ^{29}Now, Lord, consider their threats and enable your servants to speak your word with great boldness. ^{30}Stretch out your hand to heal and perform miraculous signs and wonders through the name of your holy servant Jesus." ^{31}After they prayed, the place where they were meeting was shaken. And they were all filled with the Holy Spirit and spoke the word of God boldly.

After dealing with those hostile people the apostles expected God to respond. They prayed fully expecting a show of force. They expected new power to face the enemy. They were excited to be a part of the Christ crowd. Are you? Then raise your expectations and your level of excitement. You are a winner!

An Agenda

The agenda is very closely attached to attitude. What is your motive for being in his presence? Why are you here? If you are expecting something, it does not always have to be a surprise. When you see the word agenda you may be shocked. Who sets the agenda for God? Are we not supposed to be following his agenda for our lives? The answer is yes, of course we are. But the agenda I am speaking of is a road map for you to follow so that your prayer life has purposeful intent. In the following chapters we will go into detail about the agenda or roadmap, but let me give you a sneak preview of what to expect.

Many Christians go into a prayer without a clue about what to say or how to say it. Paul writes to us in Romans 8:26 that the Holy Spirit helps us with our prayers. The Holy Spirit is a teacher, counselor, revealer of the Word, and the person who reminds us of what we have heard from God. If he reminds us then we will have had knowledge of the thing in the first place. The disciples asked Jesus to teach them how to pray. He gave them a model, a roadmap, an agenda. This is the guide you follow when you pray. It was the beginner's training guide to prayer. We know this because Jesus prays in John 17 and uses some of the agenda, but goes deeper. He intercedes for the disciples. In Acts 4, the apostles, having matured into officers of the kingdom, not just corporals and privates, boldly pray. It is an intimate expectant prayer that is beyond the basic training of Matthew 6:9-13.

One of the tools I personally use is the "CTP" method when I am reading my devotional bible. I put these letters next to verses that speak to me as I read them. "C" stands for confessions. If you read something that strikes you or convicts you in an area of your life where you see needs transforming, then confess the sin or shortcoming before God.

On the other hand, the confession may be one of confessing the Word over your life as an empowering, encouraging, life altering message to your flesh from your spirit man. For example, "I am the righteousness of God, in Christ Jesus, I am blessed coming in and blessed going out…, I do not have the spirit of fear, but power, love, and a sound mind. I have the mind of Christ. The wisdom of God is in me and I operate in it." Whenever you read something turn it into a positive confession over your life.

Make sure you read that confession at least three times. It is very important to get that in your spirit. When I read something in scripture that has happened to me or that I have been delivered from I put a "T" next to it to pray a prayer of thanksgiving. When I read about the shedding of blood and the cross Jesus bore for my sins, I put a "T" to pray a prayer of thanksgiving applying it to the scriptures I read.

"P" stands for praise. This is obviously a place I see the names of God or a place I expect God to show Himself as Shammah, Nissi, Shalom, El Elyon, etc. Praise is an acknowledgement of the person and personality of our Father. It acknowledges by history and in faith, His ability to be and do any and everything I need him to be or do in my life. It also reminds my spirit man of the power in me. If I am my Father's child, then His DNA is in me. I have his character, His blood type. No wonder "I can do all things through Christ who strengthens me." Phil. 4:19

In the remaining chapters we will follow an agenda, model, and map for prayer following the articles found in the Old Testament Tabernacle. I first encountered it some years ago studying the life of David Yonggi Cho of South Korea. As I prayed this model I learned to pray for hours at a time. It helped me to focus on areas and not just scatter gun, pop up praying.

Chapter 7

"Praying Through the Temple- The Outer Court"

Pray the following and let it guide you to worship God in the Tabernacle

The Brazen Altar – The Place of Imputed Righteousness

Imputed is defined as to charge; to attribute; to set to the account of God's righteousness which is Christ's. Christ's is imputed to us; so that God is at once "just and the justifier of him that believeth in Jesus" (Romans 3:25-26). God, in fact, deals with us all as a guilty race; for we are all liable to suffering and death; the doctrine of imputation of Adam's sin accounts for it: that of Christ's righteousness to us (Romans 5:19; 2 Corinthians 5:19; 2 Corinthians 5:21). God "hath made Him to be sin for us who knew no sin, that we might be made the righteousness of God in Him." Therefore for Christians the righteousness of Jesus Christ satisfies all criteria necessary to share in God's grace. See the Tabernacle Courtyard in your mind. See the Brazen Altar. Remember the different offerings presented at the Brazen Altar: sin, trespass, burnt offerings, thanks and reconciliation. These foretold of the sacrifice of Jesus Christ at Calvary. Recognize the tremendous cost of sin. The blood of Jesus Christ replaces the blood of animals; one sacrifice for all time through Jesus Christ. My sins are forgiven; I am declared righteous through the Cross. Father, give me sanctification and fullness of the Holy Spirit through the blood of

Jesus. Any hold that the world or the devil has on me is cancelled and broken right now in Jesus' name! Because of the blood, I am free!

    A. The Passover is happening now. The name *Passover* (Pesakh, meaning "skipping" or passing over) derives from the night of the Tenth Plague, when the Angel of Death saw the blood of the Passover lamb on the doorposts of the houses of Israel and "skipped over" them and did not kill their firstborn.

    B. The cross- the cross reminds us of God's act of love and atonement in Christ's sacrifice at Calvary - "the lamb of God who takes away the sin of the world." The cross also reminds us of Jesus' victory over sin and death, since through His death he conquered death itself. Picture yourself and declare yourself covered by the blood of Jesus and begin to thank Him for conquering death.

    C. Scriptures: The following scriptures and types are to help you launch your prayers.
    Psalm 100:4a- Enter his gates with thanksgiving and his courts with praise;

Hebrews 9:22- In fact, the law requires that nearly everything be cleansed with blood, and without the shedding of blood there is no forgiveness.

Just as blood is produced in the bone marrow and circulates through the human body to deliver nutrients and oxygen to the cells and take away waste and harmful things that "disease" us to death. Your blood Jesus does the same in the body of Christ.

1 Peter 2:24- He himself bore our sins in his body on the tree, so that we might die to sins and live for righteousness; by his wounds you have been healed.

Because my sins were washed away I owe you thanks and praise.

1. <u>Salvation:</u> Thanks for saving me Jesus. Your blood is amazing.

   A. Before I met you I was _____ (fill in your own testimony about where you were before you met the Lord, i.e. bad habits, bad relationships, etc...)
   B. Thanks for saving me from _____.
   C. According to your Word: Give Thanks for the Forgiveness of Sins.

Hebrews 9:12-14: *[12]He did not enter by means of the blood of goats and calves; but he entered the Most Holy Place once for all by his own blood, having obtained eternal redemption. [13]The blood of goats and bulls and the ashes of a heifer sprinkled on those who are ceremonially unclean sanctify them so that they are outwardly clean. [14]How much more, then, will the blood of Christ, who through the eternal Spirit offered himself unblemished to God, cleanse our consciences from acts that lead to death, so that we may serve the living God!*

Hebrews 10:4-5: *[4]because it is impossible for the blood of bulls and goats to take away sins. [5]Therefore, when Christ came into the world, he said: "Sacrifice and offering you did not desire, but a body you prepared for me;*

Hebrews 10:8-10: *[8]First he said, "Sacrifices and offerings, burnt offerings and sin offerings you did not desire, nor were you pleased with them" (although the law required them to be made). [9]Then he said, "Here I am, and I have come to do your will." He sets aside the first to establish the second. [10]And by that will, we have been made holy through the sacrifice of the body of Jesus Christ once for all.*

Psalms 51:14: *[13] Then I will teach transgressors your ways and sinners will turn back to you. [14] Save me from bloodguilt, O God, the God who saves me, and my tongue will sing of your righteousness.*

Because I am clean, saved and grateful, I promise to: _____ (what's your promise list – names to win to Christ, people to coach to a Godly, righteous life).

2. Healing:

   A. Health challenges I have experienced if any.
   B. Challenges of loved ones _____ (list them).
   C. According to your Word: Give Thanks for the Blood of Jesus

Acts 10:28 and John 10:10: [38]how God anointed Jesus of Nazareth with the Holy Spirit and power, and how he went around doing good and healing all who were under the power of the devil, because God was with him.
[10]The thief comes only to steal and kill and destroy; I have come that they may have life, and have it to the full.

I John 5:4: [4]for everyone born of God overcomes the world. This is the victory that has overcome the world, even our faith.

Luke 17:11, 14: [11]Now on his way to Jerusalem, Jesus traveled along the border between Samaria and Galilee. [14]When he saw them, he said, "Go, and show yourselves to the priests." And as they went, they were cleansed.

I Peter 12:11: [24]He himself bore our sins in his body on the tree, so that we might die to sins and live for righteousness; by his wounds you have been healed.

Revelations 12:11: [11]They overcame him by the blood of the Lamb and by the word of their testimony; they did not love their lives so much as to shrink from death.

Psalm 103:1-3: [1] Praise the LORD, O my soul; all my inmost being, praise his holy name. [2] Praise the LORD, O my soul, and forget not all his benefits- [3] who forgives all your sins and heals all your diseases.

Mark 5:1-20: ¹*They went across the lake to the region of the Gerasenes. ²When Jesus got out of the boat, a man with an evil spirit came from the tombs to meet him. ³This man lived in the tombs, and no one could bind him any more, not even with a chain. ⁴For he had often been chained hand and foot, but he tore the chains apart and broke the irons on his feet. No one was strong enough to subdue him. ⁵Night and day among the tombs and in the hills he would cry out and cut himself with stones. ⁶When he saw Jesus from a distance, he ran and fell on his knees in front of him. ⁷He shouted at the top of his voice, "What do you want with me, Jesus, Son of the Most High God? Swear to God that you won't torture me!" ⁸For Jesus had said to him, "Come out of this man, you evil spirit!" ⁹Then Jesus asked him, "What is your name?" "My name is Legion," he replied, "for we are many." ¹⁰And he begged Jesus again and again not to send them out of the area. ¹¹A large herd of pigs was feeding on the nearby hillside. ¹²The demons begged Jesus, "Send us among the pigs; allow us to go into them." ¹³He gave them permission and the evil spirits came out and went into the pigs. The herd, about two thousand in number, rushed down the steep bank into the lake and was drowned. ¹⁴Those tending the pigs ran off and reported this in the town and countryside and the people went out to see what had happened. ¹⁵When they came to Jesus, they saw the man who had been possessed by the legion of demons, sitting there, dressed and in his right mind; and they were afraid. ¹⁶Those who had seen it told the people what had happened to the demon-possessed man— and told about the pigs as well. ¹⁷Then the people began to plead with Jesus to leave their region. ¹⁸As Jesus was getting into the boat, the man who had been demon-possessed begged to go with him. ¹⁹Jesus did not let him, but said, "Go home to your family and tell them how much the Lord has done for you, and how he has had mercy on you." ²⁰So the man went away and began to tell in the Decapolis how much Jesus had done for him. And all the people were amazed.*

Luke 13:10-16: ¹⁰*On a Sabbath Jesus was teaching in one of the synagogues, ¹¹and a woman was there who had been crippled by a spirit for eighteen years. She was bent over and could not* *straighten up at all. ¹²When Jesus saw her, he called her forward and said to her, "Woman, you are set free from your infirmity." ¹³Then he put his hands on her, and immediately she straightened up and praised God. ¹⁴Indignant because Jesus had healed on the Sabbath, the synagogue ruler said to the people, "There are six days for work. So come and be healed on those days, not on the Sabbath." ¹⁵The Lord answered him, "You hypocrites! Doesn't each of you on the Sabbath untie his ox or donkey from the stall and lead it out to give it water? ¹⁶Then should not this woman, a daughter of Abraham, whom Satan has kept bound for eighteen long years, be set free on the Sabbath day from what bound her?"*

Because I am healed, I'm grateful and I owe you. Things I could not do I will do now. Thank you for straightening up my life. I can see myself free and now able to _____.

3. Curses and Deliverance

   A. Generational curses- (Generational curses are judgments that are passed on to individuals because of sins perpetuated in a family in a number of generations. They bring judgment or bondage during an individual's life, reducing the quality of life, until that individual addresses the sin issues that put the curses into place.)

   B. Meditate on issues passed down from your parents and grandparents that you or your family has struggled with.

      - Call the curses out and begin to call yourself free from each of them.
      - See the blood of Jesus cleansing and covering you. Thank him now.
      - Think about things you have possibly done that may be passed on to your children and children's children. Thank Jesus for his blood that breaks the bondage. Call your children free. The curses broken according to the word.

Read Col 3:13, 14 – Father I forgive my dad/mom/grandparents/who passed down anything on my life. Help me to free myself from any anger. Help me to love them I have hated.

1 Peter 2:19:
… it is commendable if a man bears up under the pain of unjust suffering because he is conscious of God.

C. According to Your Word:

Revelation 12:9-11:
[9]*The great dragon was hurled down—that ancient serpent called the devil, or Satan, who leads the whole world astray. He was hurled to the earth, and his angels with him.* [10]*Then I heard a loud voice in heaven say:*
"Now have come the salvation and the power and the kingdom of our God, and the authority of his Christ. For the accuser of our brothers, who accuses them before our God day and night, has been hurled down.
[11]*They overcame him by the blood of the Lamb and by the word of their testimony; they did not love their lives so much as to shrink from death.*

Lord I Thank you that because of the blood of Jesus over my life I am an overcomer. Satan is a defeated foe. I am free from bondage. My chains are broken. My wounds are healed. The Sins of my father were the sins of my grandfather's. But I am free from them all. (Even if your freedom has not manifested yet, declare it until you see it.)

Matthew 16:18:
[18]*And I tell you that you are Peter, and on this rock I will build my church and the gates of Hades will not overcome it.* I am the Church.

I thank you Father that because of the blood and my confession of Christ, the Anointed One and His Anointing, I have power that cannot be contended with by Hell. I am a winner.

1 Corinthians 15:20-26:
[20] But Christ has indeed been raised from the dead, the first fruits of those who have fallen asleep. [21] For since death came through a man, the resurrection of the dead comes also through a man. [22] For as in Adam all die, so in Christ all will be made alive. [23] But each in his own turn: Christ, the first fruits; then, when he comes, those who belong to him. [24] Then the end will come, when he hands over the kingdom to God the Father after he has destroyed all dominion, authority and power. [25] For he must reign until he has put all his enemies under his feet. [26] The last enemy to be destroyed is death.

Thank you Lord, because of your Blood, I have even over come death and the grave. I do not fear death. I know my body will die. I expect it, unless you come first. But I have joy in knowing that my spirit has an eternal home with you. Neither death, nor the grave can hold me.

    4. Protection

        A. People, plans and things I have feared (name them and cast them down).
        B. Things fear stopped me from doing or becoming.
- as a person
- in my family
- on my job/profession
- places to see

        C. According to your Word

Psalm 91
[1] He who dwells in the shelter of the Most High will rest in the shadow of the Almighty.
[2] *I will say* of the LORD, "He is my refuge and my fortress, my God, in whom I trust."
[3] Surely he will save me from the fowler's snare and from the deadly pestilence.

⁴ He will cover me with his feathers, and under his wings you will find refuge; his faithfulness will be your shield and rampart.
⁵ I will not fear the terror of night, nor the arrow that flies by day,
⁶ nor the pestilence that stalks in the darkness, nor the plague that destroys at midday.
⁷ A thousand may fall at my side, ten thousand at my right hand, but it will not come near me.
⁸ You will only observe with your eyes and see the punishment of the wicked.
⁹I have made the Most High my dwelling— even the LORD, who is my refuge-
¹⁰ then no harm will befall me; no disaster will come near my tent.
¹¹ For he will command his angels concerning me to guard me in all my ways;
¹² they will lift me up in their hands, so that I will not strike my foot against a stone.
¹³ I will tread upon the lion and the cobra; I will trample the great lion and the serpent.
¹⁴ "Because he loves me," says the LORD, "I will rescue him; I will protect him, for he acknowledges my name.
¹⁵ He will call upon me, and I will answer him; I will be with him in trouble, I will deliver him and honor him.
¹⁶ With long life will I satisfy him and show him my salvation."

II Timothy 2:7 {KJV}: *⁷For God hath not given us the spirit of fear; but of power, and of love, and of a sound mind.*

I confess that I have power, love and a sound mind.

Thank for that according to 1 John 4:4, greater is He that is in me than he that is in the world.

Hebrews 1:14 *Are not all angels ministering spirits sent to serve those who will inherit salvation?*

I have help I cannot even see. I'm never alone because I inherited salvation, because of the blood of Jesus in my life Angel's minister to me. Thanks Father – Angels I need your help with —.

5. Benefits/Blessings

According to Your Word:

Galatians 3:13-14
[13] Christ redeemed us from the curse of the law by becoming a curse for us, for it is written: "Cursed is everyone who is hung on a tree." [14] He redeemed us in order that the blessing given to Abraham might come to the Gentiles through Christ Jesus, so that by faith we might receive the promise of the Spirit.

Father I bless you for the Curse Breaker Jesus. Jesus I love you, I appreciate your obedience on the Cross that saved my life. Your blood made its difference in my life.

   A. According to **Psalm 103:1-5**, I have 6 benefits to my relationship that I cannot forget:

[1] Praise the LORD, O my soul; all my inmost being, praise his holy name. [2] Praise the LORD, O my soul, and forget not all his benefits- [3] who <u>forgives all</u> your <u>sins</u> and <u>heals all</u> your <u>diseases</u>, [4] who <u>redeems</u> your <u>life from the pit</u> and <u>crowns</u> you <u>with love and compassion</u>, [5] who <u>satisfies your</u> <u>desires with good things</u> so <u>that</u> your <u>youth is renewed like the eagle's</u>.

   B. According to **1 Peter 2:24**, I praise you for
[24] He himself bore our sins in his body on the tree, so that we might die to sins and live for righteousness; by his wounds you have been healed.

   C. I declare today that I am blessed, according to your Word.

Deuteronomy 28:1-14 says:
[1] If you fully obey the LORD your God and carefully follow all his commands I give you today, the LORD your God will set you high

above all the nations on earth. ² *All these blessings will come upon you and accompany you if you obey the LORD your God:*
³ *You will be blessed in the city and blessed in the country.*
⁴ *The fruit of your womb will be blessed, and the crops of your land and the young of your livestock—the calves of your herds and the lambs of your flocks.*
⁵ *Your basket and your kneading trough will be blessed.*
⁶ *You will be blessed when you come in and blessed when you go out.*
⁷ *The LORD will grant that the enemies who rise up against you will be defeated before you. They will come at you from one direction but flee from you in seven.*
⁸ *The LORD will send a blessing on your barns and on everything you put your hand to. The LORD your God will bless you in the land he is giving you.*
⁹ *The LORD will establish you as his holy people, as he promised you on oath, if you keep the commands of the LORD your God and walk in his ways.* ¹⁰ *Then all the peoples on earth will see that you are called by the name of the LORD, and they will fear you.* ¹¹ *The LORD will grant you abundant prosperity—in the fruit of your womb, the young of your livestock and the crops of your ground—in the land he swore to your forefathers to give you.*
¹² *The LORD will open the heavens, the storehouse of his bounty, to send rain on your land in season and to bless all the work of your hands. You will lend to many nations but will borrow from none.* ¹³ *The LORD will make you the head, not the tail. If you pay attention to the commands of the LORD your God that I give you this day and carefully follow them, you will always be at the top, never at the bottom.* ¹⁴ *Do not turn aside from any of the commands I give you today, to the right or to the left, following other gods and serving them.*

> D. I receive my blessings now as an obedient, blood brought child of God.

Thank you Lord that **Deuteronomy 8:18** says:
¹⁸ *But remember the LORD your God, for it is he who gives you the ability to produce wealth, and so confirms his covenant, which he swore to your forefathers, as it is today.*

> I am blessed today with the ability to produce wealth. It is in my DNA. I am a wealth producer. I do it to establish the Kingdom of my Father.

Proverbs 10:22: *²² The blessing of the LORD brings wealth, and he adds no trouble to it.*

> Wealth is following me. Sweat less victories are a required part of my life.

Psalm 35:27: *²⁷ May those who delight in my vindication shout for joy and gladness; may they always say, "The LORD be exalted, who delights in the well-being of his servant."*

Colossians 3:10:
¹⁰and have put on the new self, which is being renewed in knowledge in the image of its Creator.

> Because my curses are broken and I am now delivered, I am pursuing my rightful place, as one who is gaining knowledge, so I can live in the image of God.

The Laver – The Place of Introspection and Transparency

Introspection means an examination of ones strengths and feeling. Transparency means being capable of transmitting light so that images beyond can be clearly perceived.[7] Here, we clean our consciences every day like taking a bath or shower. The priests wash their hands, feet and face at the Laver. It is a looking glass. Before going into the Holy Place, look at you in the Laver –what is wrong in my heart? Desire a clear conscience. I cannot drag my guilty conscience into your presence, Lord. You won't allow it. My desire is for purity, so that I become a light carrier to offer others the ability to see God.

> A. Now Father, help me to take an honest look at me. What areas do I need help with? John 9:31 says - *³¹We know that*

God does not listen to sinners. He listens to the godly man who does his will.

B. First I want to pray for people who have offended me.

Hebrews 12:14:
[14]Make every effort to live in peace with all men and to be holy; without holiness no one will see the Lord.

Psalm 24:4:
[4] He who has clean hands and a pure heart, who does not lift up his soul to an idol or swear by what is false.

Matthew 6:14 teaches me - *[14]For if you forgive men when they sin against you, your heavenly Father will also forgive you.*

— I need your forgiveness so I can forgive every person who has offended me (call their names).

Now Lord, if I have fallen short in any area, I know you will hear me and forgive me.

C. Remove all masks.

2 Corinthians 3:17-18: *[17]Now the Lord is the Spirit, and where the Spirit of the Lord is, there is freedom. [18]And we, who with unveiled faces all reflect the Lord's glory, are being transformed into his likeness with ever-increasing glory, which comes from the Lord, who is the Spirit.*

2 Corinthians 4:1-2: *[1]Therefore, since through God's mercy we have this ministry, we do not lose heart. [2]Rather, we have renounced secret and shameful ways; we do not use deception, nor do we distort the word of God. On the contrary, by setting forth the truth plainly we commend ourselves to every man's conscience in the sight of God.*

D. Father, help me to take an honest look at the areas I need help with.

    1. Confess your sins: **Sin List- (See Appendix B)**
    2. Be honest about any that you struggle with.
    3. See yourself cleansed of every one of them.

E. *Psalm 51:1-13:*

¹ *Have mercy on me, O God, according to your unfailing love; according to your great compassion blot out my transgressions.* ² *Wash away all my iniquity and cleanse me from my sin.* ³ *For I know my transgressions, and my sin is always before me.* ⁴ *Against you, you only, have I sinned and done what is evil in your sight, so that you are proved right when you speak and justified when you judge.* ⁵ *Surely I was sinful at birth, sinful from the time my mother conceived me.* ⁶ *Surely you desire truth in the inner parts; you teach me wisdom in the inmost place.* ⁷ *Cleanse me with hyssop, and I will be clean; wash me, and I will be whiter than snow.* ⁸ *Let me hear joy and gladness; let the bones you have crushed rejoice.* ⁹ *Hide your face from my sins and blot out all my iniquity.* ¹⁰ *Create in me a pure heart, O God, and renew a steadfast spirit within me.* ¹¹ *Do not cast me from your presence or take your Holy Spirit from me.* ¹² *Restore to me the joy of your salvation and grant me a willing spirit, to sustain me.* ¹³ *Then I will teach transgressors your ways, and sinners will turn back to you.*

F. Now there are five areas I wish to address to keep order in my life
    1. <u>Righteousness</u> is important to you and therefore important to me.
        a. Lord make my holy just like you. Your desire is for me to live holy, sanctified and set apart. Jesus you are my model, my standard bearer in every aspect of life.
        b. You made me righteous by your blood, now help me to live right so my actions will measure up to my name.
        c. According to your word: Confessions

1 Peter 2:9-12: *⁹But you are a chosen people, a royal priesthood, a holy nation, a people belonging to God, that you may declare the praises of him who called you out of darkness into his wonderful light. ¹⁰Once you were not a people, but now you are the people of God; once you had not received mercy, but now you have received mercy. ¹¹Dear friends, I urge you, as aliens and strangers in the world, to abstain from sinful desires, which war against your soul. ¹²Live such good lives among the pagans that, though they accuse you of doing wrong, they may see your good deeds and glorify God on the day he visits us.*

II Corinthians 5:20-21: *²⁰We are therefore Christ's ambassadors, as though God were making his appeal through us. We implore you on Christ's behalf: Be reconciled to God. ²¹God made him who had no sin to be sin for us, so that in him we might become the righteousness of God.*

I Peter 1:13-16: *¹³Therefore, prepare your minds for action; be self-controlled; set your hope fully on the grace to be given you when Jesus Christ is revealed. ¹⁴As obedient children do not conform to the evil desires you had when you lived in ignorance. ¹⁵But just as he who called you is holy, so be holy in all you do; ¹⁶for it is written: "Be holy, because I am holy."*

Proverbs 29:2: *² When the righteous thrive, the people rejoice; when the wicked rule, the people groan.*

> Because I live right before you, my family rejoices, my community and my city rejoice.

Proverbs 28:1: *¹ The wicked man flees though no one pursues, but the righteous are as bold as a lion.*

> When you made me righteous I chose to live it. I took off fear, looking over my shoulder, hiding and all that comes with sin. Mow I am bold as a lion.

Proverbs 11:3-30: *³ The integrity of the upright guides them, but the unfaithful are destroyed by their duplicity. ⁴ Wealth is* worthless in the day of wrath, but righteousness delivers from death. ⁵ The righteousness of the blameless makes a straight way for them, but the wicked are brought down by their own wickedness. ⁶ The righteousness of the upright delivers them, but the unfaithful are trapped by evil desires. ⁷ When a wicked man dies, his hope perishes; all he expected from his power comes to nothing. ⁸ The righteous man is rescued from trouble, and it comes on the wicked instead. ⁹ With his mouth the godless destroy his neighbor, but through knowledge the righteous escape. ¹⁰ When the righteous prosper, the city rejoices; when the wicked perish, there are shouts of joy. ¹¹ Through the blessing of the upright a city is exalted, but by the mouth of the wicked it is destroyed. ¹² A man who lacks judgment derides his neighbor, but a man of understanding holds his tongue. ¹³ A gossip betrays a confidence, but a trustworthy man keeps a secret. ¹⁴ For lack of guidance a nation falls, but many advisers make victory sure. ¹⁵ He who puts up security for another will surely suffer, but whoever refuses to strike hands in pledge is safe. ¹⁶ A kindhearted woman gains respect, but ruthless men gain only wealth. ¹⁷ A kind man benefits himself, but a cruel man brings trouble on himself. ¹⁸ The wicked man earns deceptive wages, but he who sows righteousness reaps a sure reward. ¹⁹ The truly righteous man attains life, but he who pursues evil goes to his death. ²⁰ The LORD detests men of perverse heart but he delights in those whose ways are blameless. ²¹ Be sure of this: The wicked will not go unpunished, but those who are righteous will go free. ²² Like a gold ring in a pig's snout is a beautiful woman who shows no discretion. ²³ The desire of the righteous ends only in good, but the hope of the wicked only in wrath. ²⁴ One man gives freely, yet gains even more; another withholds unduly, but comes to poverty. ²⁵ A generous man will prosper; he who refreshes others will himself be refreshed. ²⁶ People curse the man who hoards grain, but blessing crowns him who is willing to sell. ²⁷ He who seeks good finds goodwill, but evil comes to him who searches for it. ²⁸ Whoever trusts in his riches will fall, but the righteous will thrive like a green leaf. ²⁹ He who brings trouble on his family will inherit only wind, and the fool will be servant to the wise. ³⁰ The fruit of the righteous is a tree of life, and he who wins souls is wise.

2. Honesty

    A. Jesus you said you were the way, the truth and the life. You live in me; therefore I desire to live out who lives in me.
    B. Satan is called the father of lies (John 8:44). So if I am dishonest, then I acknowledge another father. I am a child of God alone. Jesus you are my savior. You teach me to speak the truth in love (Ephesians 4:15). Help me to always do just that.
    C. According to Your Word

Proverbs 12:14: *[14] From the fruit of his lips a man is filled with good things as surely as the work of his hands rewards him.*

Proverbs 5:6: *[6] She gives no thought to the way of life; her paths are crooked, but she knows it not.*

Psalm 24:12-16: *[12] Whoever of you loves life and desires to see many good days, [13] keep your tongue from evil and your lips from speaking lies. [14] Turn from evil and do good; seek peace and pursue it. [15] The eyes of the LORD are on the righteous and his ears are attentive to their cry; [16] the face of the LORD is against those who do evil, to cut off the memory of them from the earth.*

Proverbs 12:22: *[22] The LORD detests lying lips, but he delights in men who are truthful.*

II Corinthians 4:1-2: *[1] Therefore, since through God's mercy we have this ministry, we do not lose heart. [2] Rather, we have renounced secret and shameful ways; we do not use deception, nor do we distort the word of God. On the contrary, by setting forth the truth plainly we commend ourselves to every man's conscience in the sight of God.*

3. Humility

   A. When I think about all I have done and who I have been and that person who I have become, am becoming, and will be; it makes me bow down and appreciate you more. How could I take this lightly? All I am is because of you.
   B. Things I have tried to carry the weight of when it wasn't mine to carry. Situations I tried to handle when I claimed you were Lord of my life (list them). Forgive me Lord. I submit my total will to you.
   C. According to Your Word

Proverbs 8:13: [13] *To fear the LORD is to hate evil; I hate pride and arrogance, evil behavior and perverse speech.*

> You hate pride; therefore I will not have it in me or around me.

Proverbs 13:10: [10] *Pride only breeds quarrels, but wisdom is found in those who take advice.*

> Forgive me for any act of pride, arrogance, or selfishness that I have portrayed.

Proverbs 16:18: [18] *Pride goes before destruction, a haughty spirit before a fall.*

> Forgive me for only thinking of my needs and not the needs of others. For not seeking advice or counsel and wisdom in areas I lack understanding.

Proverbs 29:23: [23] *A man's pride brings him low, but a man of lowly spirit gains honor.*

> Forgive me for my stubbornness.

Proverbs 11:2: [2] *When pride comes, then comes disgrace, but with humility comes wisdom.*

Proverbs 22:4: *[4] Humility and the fear of the LORD bring wealth and honor and life.*

> You are Lord over every area of my life. I give you permission to do what you will in me and through me.

I Peter 5:5-7: *[5]Young men, in the same way be submissive to those who are older. All of you, clothe yourselves with humility toward one another, because, "God opposes the proud but gives grace to the humble." [6]Humble yourselves, therefore, under God's mighty hand, that he may lift you up in due time. [7]Cast all your anxiety on him because he cares for you.*

> I swallow my pride to apologize to people I have offended instead of waiting for them to approach me with the offense.

4. <u>Faithfulness/Loyalty</u>

   A. Forgive me for letting you down in any area of my life. Forgive me for not being loyal to you in word or deed in private and public.
   B. If I have not made you Lord over my heart and my mouth, show me how to give you full control. Convict me every time I stray.
   C. Father, my desire is to walk in "sonship" so that you can be proud of me as you were of Jesus. He never wavered and you never wondered about where He stood. I want to be like Jesus. Help Me!
   D. Areas I need help in to be faithful where I am planted:

      i. Marriage (if married)
      ii. Single – to be faithful at living holy. Forgive me if I sinned in the past. Restore my purity. Make me an example before others.

- iii. Parenting – teach me to instruct my children. To love them like you love me and model Godly parenting to others.
- iv. Job – that I do my work as unto you, with excellence. That I see my job as an opportunity to witness in the world.
- v. Ministry gifts used – that I exercise my gifts to your glory.
- vi. Prayer/Word – loyal, faithful to our fellowship time so I can hear your instructions for me.
- vii. Evangelism/Discipleship – people I'm assigned to; show me how.
- viii. Stewardship of finances – budgeting my money, living with my means. Faithful tither, loyal in sowing into the Kingdom, people, places or things.

E. According to your Word:

Proverbs 3:5-7: *[5] Trust in the LORD with all your heart and lean not on your own understanding; [6] in all your ways acknowledge him, and he will make your paths straight. [7] Do not be wise in your own eyes; fear the LORD and shun evil.*

I Corinthians 4:2: *[2] Now it is required that those who have been given a trust must prove faithful.*

Galatians 2:20: *[20] I have been crucified with Christ and I no longer live, but Christ lives in me. The life I live in the body, I live by faith in the Son of God, who loved me and gave himself for me.*

Proverbs 11:29: *[29] He who brings trouble on his family will inherit only wind, and the fool will be servant to the wise.*

Proverbs 22:6-7, 15: *[6] Train a child in the way he should go, and when he is old he will not turn from it. [7] The rich rule over the poor, and the borrower is servant to the lender. [15] Folly is bound up in the heart of a child, but the rod of discipline will drive it far from him.*

Colossians 3:17-24: [17]*And whatever you do, whether in word or deed, do it all in the name of the Lord Jesus, giving thanks to God the Father through him.* [18]*Wives, submit to your husbands, as is fitting in the Lord.* [19]*Husbands, love your wives and do not be harsh with them.* [20]*Children, obey your parents in everything, for this pleases the Lord.* [21]*Fathers, do not embitter your children, or they will become discouraged.* [22]*Slaves, obey your earthly masters in everything; and do it, not only when their eye is on you and to win their favor, but with sincerity of heart and reverence for the Lord.* [23]*Whatever you do, work at it with all your heart, as working for the Lord, not for men,* [24]*since you know that you will receive an inheritance from the Lord as a reward. It is the Lord Christ you are serving.*

Matthew 28:19-20: [19]*Therefore go and make disciples of all nations, baptizing them in the name of the Father and of the Son and of the Holy Spirit,* [20]*and teaching them to obey everything I have commanded you. And surely I am with you always, to the very end of the age."*

Malachi 3:8-12: [8] *"Will a man rob God? Yet you rob me. "But you ask, 'How do we rob you?' "In tithes and offerings.* [9] *You are under a curse—the whole nation of you—because you are robbing me.* [10] *Bring the whole tithe into the storehouse, that there may be food in my house. Test me in this," says the LORD Almighty, "and see if I will not throw open the floodgates of heaven and pour out so much blessing that you will not have room enough for it.* [11] *I will prevent pests from devouring your crops, and the vines in your fields will not cast their fruit," says the LORD Almighty.* [12] *"Then all the nations will call you blessed, for yours will be a delightful land," says the LORD Almighty.*

II Corinthians 9:6-15 {MSG}: [6-7]*Remember: A stingy planter gets a stingy crop; a lavish planter gets a lavish crop. I want each of you to take plenty of time to think it over, and make up your own mind what you will give. That will protect you against sob stories and arm-twisting. God loves it when the giver delights in the giving.* [8-11]*God can pour on the blessings in astonishing ways so that you're ready for anything and everything, more than just* *ready to do what needs to be done. As one psalmist puts it, He throws caution to the winds, giving to the needy in reckless abandon. His right-living, right-giving ways never run out, never wear out. This most generous God who gives seed to the farmer that becomes bread for your meals is more than extravagant with you. He gives you something you can then give away, which grows into full-formed lives, robust in God, wealthy in every way, so that you can be generous in every way, producing with us great praise to God. [12-15] Carrying out this social relief work involves far more than helping meet the bare needs of poor Christians. It also produces abundant and bountiful thanksgivings to God. This relief offering is a prod to live at your very best, showing your gratitude to God by being openly obedient to the plain meaning of the Message of Christ. You show your gratitude through your generous offerings to your needy brothers and sisters, and really toward everyone. Meanwhile, moved by the extravagance of God in your lives, they'll respond by praying for you in passionate intercession for whatever you need. Thank God for this gift, his gift. No language can praise it enough!*

5. <u>Love:</u>

    a. Father, help me to love the people I have forgiven, that have offended me.
    b. People who offended me in my past (list them).
    c. Secrets in my life that have made me emotionally sick. People who I allow to "push my button" and get me out of my spiritual character.
    d. According to your Word:

Galatians 5:6: *[6] For in Christ Jesus neither circumcision nor uncircumcision has any value. The only thing that counts is faith expressing itself through love.*

I know my faith can't work for me without love, so teach me to love like you loved me on the cross.

Matthew 22:37-39: *[37] Jesus replied: "'Love the Lord your God with all your heart and with all your soul and with all your mind.' [38] This is the first and greatest commandment. [39] And the second is like it: 'Love your neighbor as yourself.'*

Matthew 5:44: *[44]But I tell you: Love your enemies and pray for those who persecute you...*

Proverbs 3:3: *[3] Let love and faithfulness never leave you; bind them around your neck, write them on the tablet of your heart.*

John 15:12: *[12]My command is this: Love each other as I have loved you.*

Romans 12:9: *[9]Love must be sincere. Hate what is evil; cling to what is good.*

Romans 13:10: *[10]Love does no harm to its neighbor. Therefore love is the fulfillment of the law.*

I Corinthians 8:1: *[1]Now about food sacrificed to idols: We know that we all possess knowledge. Knowledge puffs up, but love builds up.*

I Corinthians 13:4-8: *[4]Love is patient, love is kind. It does not envy, it does not boast, it is not proud. [5]It is not rude, it is not self-seeking, it is not easily angered, and it keeps no record of wrongs. [6]Love does not delight in evil but rejoices with the truth. [7]It always protects, always trusts, always hopes, always perseveres. [8]Love never fails. But where there are prophecies, they will cease; where there are tongues, they will be stilled; where there is knowledge, it will pass away.*

> I thank you Father, for loving me when I was unlovely. Thank you for loving me enough to wash away every one of my sins. Thanks for teaching me to love in spite of the unlovely in others. I am not accountable for their actions, but I am accountable for mine. You loved me while I was in my sins. Now that I know that, I can love others while they are in theirs. I release forgiveness now for _____ (name people). I thank you for removing the burden of anger, hatred, competition, fear, superiority and unnecessary weight of frustration that was stealing my ability to live life to the fullest. I fully

expect that excess baggage has been removed from my life. I am free to experience divine health and wealth, physically, emotionally, spiritually and financially. Glory to your Name God.

Chapter 8

"Praying Through the Temple - The Inner Court"

Golden Candlestick – The Place of Impartation

To impart means to communicate the knowledge of something; to make known by words or tokens; to share. When Paul shares with the Church of Rome, "That I may impart unto you some spiritual gift (Romans 1:11) he shares with them the hope that they would increase in faith and love through his teachings and influence of his life being lived before them. The candlesticks, symbolic of the Holy Spirit, the sevenfold Spirit of God: wisdom, understanding, counsel, might, knowledge, fear of the Lord and holiness. Holy Spirit, I welcome a deeper more intimate relationship with you today. Dear Holy Spirit, give me your wisdom. Help me to solve all the problems I face through your wisdom. Give me your understanding so that I may understand the deep truths of God, and I may live those truths and pass them on to my children. Give me counsel so that I will follow your narrow path.

   A. Pray this prayer, *II Corinthians 13:17-18,* *"^{17}Now the Lord is the Spirit, and where the Spirit of the Lord is, there is freedom. ^{18}And we, who with unveiled faces all reflect the Lord's glory, are being transformed into his likeness with ever-increasing glory, which comes from the Lord, who is the Spirit"*

B. I'm Inspired by the presence as I take off my masks- I see Him- Light returns to me- The eyes of my understanding are open- ***2 Kings 6:17:****And Elisha prayed, "O LORD, open his eyes so he may see." Then the LORD opened the servant's eyes, and he looked and saw the hills full of horses and chariots of fire all around Elisha.*

C. Holy Spirit, I acknowledge you and thank you for who you are.

> You are <u>wisdom</u> – help me to see everything like you see it and do all according to your word.
>
> You are my <u>counselor</u> – guide me so I can guide others to you. Open my ears to hear your voice above all others.
>
> You keep <u>bringing to my remembrance</u> the Word so I can live as a kingdom-ambassador.
>
> You give me <u>power</u> to break yokes with knowledge of the word. ***II Corinthians 10:4-5:*** *⁴The weapons we fight with are not the weapons of the world. On the contrary, they have divine power to demolish strongholds. ⁵We demolish arguments and every pretension that sets itself up against the knowledge of God and we take captive every thought to make it obedient to Christ.*
>
> You are my <u>fruit-bearer</u>.
>
> You are my <u>gift-giver</u>.

1. <u>Spiritual Gifts</u> (Romans 12:6-8, 1 Corinthians 12:4-11, Ephesians 4:11)

> Word of wisdom
> Apostles
> Word of knowledge

Teachers/teaching
Faith
Helps/helping
Gift of healing
Administrations/guidance
Miracles/miraculous powers
Ministry/serving
Prophecy
Encouragement/exhortation
Discernment of Spirits
Giving
Speaking in tongues
Leading
Interpretation of tongues
Showing Mercy
Evangelists
Pastors

   a. Gifts I have _____.
   b. Gifts I desire _____. (For what purpose?)
   c. According to your word:

I am available to be used any way you desire. I realize that what I have is a gift from you. You deserve the glory for the outcome of everything I say and do.

I Corinthians 12:12-20: *[12] The body is a unit, though it is made up of many parts; and though all its parts are many, they form one body. So it is with Christ. [13] For we were all baptized by one Spirit into one body—whether Jews or Greeks, slave or free—and we were all given the one Spirit to drink. [14] Now the body is not made up of one part but of many. [15] If the foot should say, "Because I am not a hand, I do not belong to the body," it would not for that reason cease to be part of the body. [16] And if the ear should say, "Because I am not an eye, I do not belong to the body," it would not for that reason cease to be part of the body. [17] If the whole body* were an eye, where would the sense of hearing be? If the whole body were an ear, where would the sense of smell be? [18]But in fact God has arranged the parts in the body, every one of them, just as he wanted them to be. [19]If they were all one part, where would the body be? [20]As it is, there are many parts, but one body.

I am a part of the body of Christ

John 14:26 But the Counselor, the Holy Spirit, whom the Father will send in my name, will teach you all things and will remind you of everything I have said to you.

Acts 1:8: But you will receive power when the Holy Spirit comes on you; and you will be my witnesses in Jerusalem, and in all Judea and Samaria, and to the ends of the earth."

Acts 2:4: All of them were filled with the Holy Spirit and began to speak in other tongues [Or languages; also in verse 11] as the Spirit enabled them.

Romans 8:26: In the same way, the Spirit helps us in our weakness. We do not know what we ought to pray for, but the Spirit himself intercedes for us with groans that words cannot express.

John 16:7-11: [7]But I tell you the truth: It is for your good that I am going away. Unless I go away, the Counselor will not come to you; but if I go, I will send him to you. [8]When he comes, he will convict the world of guilt in regard to sin and righteousness and judgment: [9]in regard to sin, because men do not believe in me; [10]in regard to righteousness, because I am going to the Father, where you can see me no longer; [11]and in regard to judgment, because the prince of this world now stands condemned

2. <u>Spiritual fruit</u>

a. As fruit helps to nourish the physical body with its sweetness and substance, so it is with your fruit, my life will be enhanced as I nurture your fruit in my life.

      b. Lord help me not to be satisfied with some fruit active in me, but all. Help me to use my fruit to activate my gifts so that I do not fail to show others who you are.
      c. According to your word.

Galatians 5:22-23: *²²But the fruit of the Spirit is love, joy, peace, patience, kindness, goodness, faithfulness, ²³gentleness and self-control. Against such things there is no law.*

<u>Love</u> – ***I Corinthians 13:1:*** *¹If I speak in the tongues of men and of angels, but have not love, I am only a resounding gong or a clanging cymbal.*

<u>Joy</u> – ***Psalm 45:7, 47:1-5:*** *⁷ You love righteousness and hate wickedness; therefore God, your God, has set you above your companions by anointing you with the oil of joy;*

¹ Clap your hands, all you nations; shout to God with cries of joy. ² How awesome is the LORD Most High, the great King over all the earth! ³ He subdued nations under us, peoples under our feet. ⁴ He chose our inheritance for us, the pride of Jacob, whom he loved. Selah ⁵ God has ascended amid shouts of joy, the LORD amid the sounding of trumpets.

<u>Peace</u> – ***James 3:17-18, Colossians 3:15:*** *¹⁷But the wisdom that comes from heaven is first of all pure; then peace-loving, considerate, submissive, full of mercy and good fruit, impartial and sincere. ¹⁸Peacemakers who sow in peace raise a harvest of righteousness.*

¹⁵Let the peace of Christ rule in your hearts, since as members of one body you were called to peace. And be thankful.

<u>Patience</u> – ***Hebrews 6:12, Romans 12:12:*** *¹²We do not want you to become lazy, but to imitate those who through faith and patience inherit what has been promised.*

[12] *Be joyful in hope, patient in affliction, faithful in prayer.*

<u>Kindness</u> – **Proverbs 11:17, 14:31, 19:17:** [17] *A kind man benefits himself, but a cruel man brings trouble on himself.*

[31] *He who oppresses the poor shows contempt for their Maker, but whoever is kind to the needy honors God.*

<u>Goodness</u> – **2 Thessalonians 1:11:** [11] *With this in mind, we constantly pray for you, that our God may count you worthy of his calling, and that by his power he may fulfill every good purpose of yours and every act prompted by your faith*

<u>Faithfulness</u> – **III John 5:** [5] *Dear friend, you are faithful in what you are doing for the brothers, even though they are strangers to you.*

<u>Gentleness</u> – **Proverbs 15:1:** [1] *A gentle answer turns away wrath, but a harsh word stirs up anger.*

<u>Self-control</u> – **I Peter 5:8:** [8] *Be self-controlled and alert. Your enemy the devil prowls around like a roaring lion looking for someone to devour.*

II Peter 1:3-8, 10: [3] *His divine power has given us everything we need for life and godliness through our knowledge of him who called us by his own glory and goodness.* [4] *Through these he has given us his very great and precious promises, so that through them you may participate in the divine nature and escape the corruption in the world caused by evil desires.* [5] *For this very reason, make every effort to add to your faith goodness; and to goodness, knowledge;* [6] *and to knowledge, self-control; and to self-control, perseverance; and to perseverance, godliness;* [7] *and to godliness, brotherly kindness; and to brotherly kindness, love.* [8] *For if you possess these qualities in increasing measure, they will keep you from being ineffective and unproductive in your knowledge of our Lord Jesus Christ.* [10] *Therefore, my brothers, be all the more eager to make your calling and election sure. For if you do these things, you will never fall...*

Lord help me to add to *me* the things you desire so that *I* can live the life that will please you. I recognize that I *am* you in the earth.

Holy Spirit, I love you. I desire an intimate relationship with you. I want to know you and I give you permission to have full control of all of my faculties. Help me so that I will never embarrass my dad, but imitate him in such a way, that the glory shows up when I do.

3. Confessions:

I am the temple in which you dwell today (1 Corinthians 3:16).

My body is the place where your ark dwells.

I am bought with a price and gladly yield my heart, my hands, my mind, my tongue and my feet to be used by you.

You are Lord, forever.

4. Today's Assignment:

a. Whatever I have to do today, give me wisdom. (Name the things you have to do, the people you have to meet).
b. Ask for the Harvest...Souls of the unsaved. (Psalms 2:8).
c. Lord of the Harvest, give me some people to lead to you. May I be you today so that others are convicted, convinced and become committed to you when they come in contact with me. Breathe on me again so

that I look like you when I look at me – No flesh- a fully developed spirit man.

The Shewbread- The Place of Inspiration

A. The Shewbread is the symbol of the Word of God. Thank you for your *logos* word and your Rhema word. Thank you for the written word and the inspired Word of God. All the 7,000+ promises of God are written in the scriptures. The *logos* written word is potentially mine, but not necessarily practically mine today. Rhema is inspired word made alive in my heart today for a specific application

B. Give me Lord, your specific word – your Rhema Word – for my life today. Give me this day my daily bread.

C. Jesus you are the new manna- bread of life. I anxiously sup daily and I'm made in your image.

I love your Word. It gives me life.

D. **According to your Word:**

I make these confessions over my life: *John 1:1- In the beginning was the Word, and the Word was with God, and the Word was God.*

The Word lives in me. I am a living breathing example of the Word made flesh.

Psalm 119:1-16: *[1] Blessed are they whose ways are blameless, who walk according to the law of the LORD. [2] Blessed are they who keep his statutes and seek him with all their heart. [3] They do nothing wrong; they walk in his ways. [4] You have laid down precepts that are to be fully obeyed. [5] Oh, that my ways were steadfast*
in obeying your decrees! [6] Then I would not be put to shame when I consider all your commands. [7] I will praise you with an

upright heart as I learn your righteous laws. [8] I will obey your decrees; do not utterly forsake me. [9] How can a young man keep his way pure? By living according to your word. [10] I seek you with all my heart; do not let me stray from your commands. [11] I have hidden your word in my heart that I might not sin against you. [12] Praise be to you, O LORD; teach me your decrees. [13] With my lips I recount all the laws that come from your mouth. [14] I rejoice in following your statutes as one rejoices in great riches. [15] I meditate on your precepts and consider your ways. [16] I delight in your decrees; I will not neglect your word.

Psalm 119:18-20: [18] Open my eyes that I may see wonderful things in your law. [19] I am a stranger on earth; do not hide your commands from me. [20] My soul is consumed with longing for your laws at all times.

Psalm 119:24-28: [24] Your statutes are my delight; they are my counselors. [25] I am laid low in the dust; preserve my life according to your word. [26] I recounted my ways and you answered me; teach me your decrees. [27] Let me understand the teaching of your precepts; then I will meditate on your wonders. [28] My soul is weary with sorrow; strengthen me according to your word

Psalm 119:37: Turn my eyes away from worthless things; preserve my life according to your word.

Psalm 119:40: How I long for your precepts! Preserve my life in your righteousness.

Psalm 119:43-48: [43] Do not snatch the word of truth from my mouth, for I have put my hope in your laws. [44] I will always obey your law, forever and ever. [45] I will walk about in freedom, for I have sought out your precepts. [46] I will speak of your statutes before kings and will not be put to shame, [47] for I delight in your commands because I love them. [48] I lift up my hands to your commands, which I love, and I meditate on your decrees

Psalm 119:54-62: [54] Your decrees are the theme of my song wherever I lodge. [55] In the night I remember your name, O LORD, and I will keep your law. [56] This has been my practice: I obey your precepts. [57] You are my portion, O LORD; I have promised to obey your words. [58] I have sought your face with all my heart; be gracious to me according to your promise. [59] I have considered my ways and have turned my steps to your statutes. [60] I will hasten and not delay to obey your commands. [61] Though the wicked bind me with ropes, I will not forget your law. [62] At midnight I rise to give you thanks for your righteous laws.

Psalm 119:64: The earth is filled with your love, O LORD; teach me your decrees.

Psalm 119:89-90: [89] Your word, O LORD, is eternal; it stands firm in the heavens. [90] Your faithfulness continues through all generations; you established the earth, and it endures.

Psalm 107:20: You sent forth your word and your word healed me; you rescued me from the grave.

Genesis 1- Just as you spoke and creation happened, Empower Me to do the same. [1] In the beginning God created the heavens and the earth. [2] Now the earth was formless and empty, darkness was over the surface of the deep, and the Spirit of God was hovering over the waters. [3] And God said, "Let there be light," and there was light. [4] God saw that the light was good, and He separated the light from the darkness. [5] God called the light "day," and the darkness he called "night." And there was evening, and there was morning—the first day. [6] And God said, "Let there be an expanse between the waters to separate water from water." [7] So God made the expanse and separated the water under the expanse from the water above it. And it was so. [8] God called the expanse "sky." And there was evening, and there was morning—the second day. [9] And God said, "Let the water under the sky be gathered to one place, and let dry ground appear." And it was so. [10] God called the dry ground "land," and the gathered waters he called "seas." And God saw that it was good. [11] Then God said, "Let the land produce vegetation: seed-bearing plants and trees on the land that bear fruit with seed in it, according to their various kinds." And it was so. [12] The land produced vegetation: plants bearing *seed according to their kinds and trees bearing fruit with seed in it according to their kinds. And God saw that it was good.* [13] *And there was evening, and there was morning—the third day.* [14] *And God said, "Let there be lights in the expanse of the sky to separate the day from the night, and let them serve as signs to mark seasons and days and years,* [15] *and let them be lights in the expanse of the sky to give light on the earth." And it was so.* [16] *God made two great lights—the greater light to govern the day and the lesser light to govern the night. He also made the stars.* [17] *God set them in the expanse of the sky to give light on the earth,* [18] *to govern the day and the night, and to separate light from darkness. And God saw that it was good.* [19] *And there was evening, and there was morning—the fourth day.* [20] *And God said, "Let the water teem with living creatures, and let birds fly above the earth across the expanse of the sky."* [21] *So God created the great creatures of the sea and every living and moving thing with which the water teems, according to their kinds, and every winged bird according to its kind. And God saw that it was good.* [22] *God blessed them and said, "Be fruitful and increase in number and fill the water in the seas, and let the birds increase on the earth."* [23] *And there was evening, and there was morning—the fifth day.* [24] *And God said, "Let the land produce living creatures according to their kinds: livestock, creatures that move along the ground, and wild animals, each according to its kind." And it was so.* [25] *God made the wild animals according to their kinds, the livestock according to their kinds, and all the creatures that move along the ground according to their kinds. And God saw that it was good.* [26] *Then God said, "Let us make man in our image, in our likeness, and let them rule over the fish of the sea and the birds of the air, over the livestock, over all the earth, and over all the creatures that move along the ground."*

[27] *So God created man in his own image, in the image of God he created him; male and female he created them.* [28] *God blessed them and said to them, "Be fruitful and increase in number; fill the earth and subdue it. Rule over the fish of the sea and the birds of the air and over every living creature that moves on the ground."*

[29] *Then God said, "I give you every seed-bearing plant on the face of the whole earth and every tree that has fruit with seed in it. They will be yours for food.* [30] *And to all the beasts of the earth and all the birds of the air and all the creatures that move on the*

ground—everything that has the breath of life in it—I give every green plant for food." And it was so. ^{31} *God saw all that he had made, and it was very good. And there was evening, and there was morning—the sixth day.Give me a God-said today and then make me a God-said until I say what you say and see it come to pass like you see it; immediately.*

>Give me a God-said today and then make me a God-said until I say what you say and see it come to pass like you see it; immediately.

Revelation 12:11: *You Said, they overcame him by the blood of the Lamb and by the word of their testimony; they did not love their lives so much as to shrink from death.*

>I therefore defy the enemy with your Word and then he must flee, now.

>E. I ask for fresh bread/ revelation- **Matthew 6:11:** *Give me today my daily bread.*

>Open the eyes of my understanding as I study.
>I love to read, hear, speak and live your Word.
>I love listening to tapes. I purchase them often.
>I love reading my Bible. Everyday it brings me joy and peace.

Chapter 9

"The Incense Altar: The Place of Illumination; The Holy of Holies"

At the place of illumination or enlightenment, stand, kneel or lay prostrate for several minutes and simply praise God by singing in the Spirit or praying as the Lord would lead you (Psalm 100:4b).

A. I saw in *2 Chronicles 7:1-4:*
> [1] *When Solomon finished praying, fire came down from heaven and consumed the burnt offering and the sacrifices, and the glory of the LORD filled the temple.* [2] *The priests could not enter the temple of the LORD because the glory of the LORD filled it.* [3] *When all the Israelites saw the fire coming down and the glory of the LORD above the temple, they knelt on the pavement with their faces to the ground, and they worshiped and gave thanks to the LORD, saying,*
> *"He is good; his love endures forever."*
> [4] *Then the king and all the people offered sacrifices before the LORD.*
>
> Fill this place now with your presence (now sing Him a love song).

B. Your word says in **Psalm 100:4b:** *give thanks to him and praise his name.* I acknowledge who you are and when I call your name I am strengthened by my understanding of who You are and who You are inside of me. I am your off spring, you are my Dad, and I have your DNA in me.

I see you in me-
> **2 Corinthians 4:6-7:** *You made your light shine in my heart to give me the light of the knowledge of the glory of God in the face of Christ. This treasure in jars of clay*

C. Live in me, Breath in me, I love to call your name. According to Psalm 22:3(KJV) – You inhabit, you come to live in the praise of your people. I invite you to reside in me, make me a revelator of you. Make my heart your habitation. Be seated in my praises. Be lifted high wherever I go and I will watch the world be drawn unto you. You name is strength to me.

1. **EL**: God ("Mighty, Strong, Prominent") Gen. 7:1, 28:3, 35:11; Num. 23:22; Josh. 3:10; 2 Sam. 22:31, 32; Neh. 1:5, 9:32; Isa. 9:6; Ezek. 10:5.
ELOHIM: God as Creator, Preserver, Transcendent, Mighty and Strong. Gen. 17:7, 6:18, 9:15, 50:24; I Kings 8:23; Jer. 31:33; Isa. 40:1.
EL SHADDAI: God Almighty Or "God All Sufficient." Gen. 17:1, 2.
ADONAI: "Master" Or "Lord" Gen. 15:2.
JEHOVAH: Yahweh, YHWH Is The Covenant Name Of God. "I AM WHO I AM" Or 'I WILL BE WHO I WILL BE" (Dan. 9:14; Ps. 11:7; Lev. 19:2; Hab. 1:12).
JEHOVAH-JIREH: "The Lord Will Provide." Gen. 22:14. From "Jireh" ("To See" Or "To Provide," Or To "Foresee" As A Prophet.) God Always Provides, Adequate When The Times Come.
JEHOVAH-ROPHE: "The Lord Who Heals" Ex. 15:22-26. From "Rophe" ("To Heal"); Implies Spiritual, Emotional As Well As Physical Healing. (Jer. 30:17, 3:22; Isa. 61:1) God Heals Body, Soul And Spirit; All Levels Of Man's Being.

JEHOVAH-NISSI: *"The Lord Our Banner." Ex. 17:15. God On The Battlefield, From Word Which Means, "To Glisten," "To Lift Up," See Psalm 4:6.*
JEHOVAH-M'KADDESH: *"The Lord Who Sanctifies" Lev. 20:8. "To Make Whole, Set Apart For Holiness."*
JEHOVAH-SHALOM: *"The Lord Our Peace" Judges 6:24. "Shalom" Translated "Peace" 170 Times Means "Whole," "Finished," "Fulfilled," "Perfected." Related To "Well," Welfare." Deut. 27:6; Dan. 5:26; I Kings 9:25 8:61; Gen. 15:16; Ex. 21:34, 22:5, 6; Lev. 7:11-21. Shalom Means That Kind Of Peace That Results From Being A Whole Person In Right Relationship To God And To One's Fellow Man.*
SHEPHERD: *Psa. 23, 79:13, 95:7, 80:1, 100:3; Gen. 49:24; Isa. 40:11.*
JUDGE: *Psa. 7:8, 96:13.*
JEHOVAH ELOHIM: *"LORD God" Gen. 2:4; Judges 5:3; Isa. 17:6; Zeph. 2:9; Psa. 59:5,*
JEHOVAH-TSIDKENU *"The Lord Our Righteousness" Jer. 23:5, 6, 33:16. From "Tsidek" (Straight, Stiff, Balanced - As On Scales - Full Weight, Justice, Right, Righteous, Declared Innocent.) God Our Righteousness.*
JEHOVAH-ROHI: *"The Lord Our Shepherd" Psa. 23, From "Ro'eh" (To Pasture).*
JEHOVAH-SHAMMAH: *"The Lord Is There" (Ezek. 48:35).*
JEHOVAH-SABAOTH: *"The Lord Of Hosts" The Commander Of The Angelic Host And The Armies Of God. Isa. 1:24; Psa. 46:7, 11; 2 Kings 3:9-12; Jer. 11:20 (NT: Rom. 9:29; James 5:4, Rev. 19: 11-16).*
EL ELYON: *'Most High" (From "To Go Up") Deut. 26:19, 32:8; Psa. 18:13; Gen. 14:18; Num. 24:16; Psa. 78:35, 7:17, 18:13, 97:9, 56:2, 78:56, 18:13; Dan. 7:25, 27; Isa. 14:14.*
ABHIR: *'Mighty One', ("To Be Strong") Gen. 49:24; Deut. 10:17; Psa. 132:2, 5; Isa. 1:24, 49:26, 60:1.*
SHAPHAT: *"Judge" Gen. 18:25*

EL ROI: "*God Of Seeing*" Hagar In Gen. 16:13. The God Who Opens Our Eyes.
EYALUTH: "*Strength*" Psa. 22:19.
TSADDIQ: "*Righteous One*" Psa. 7:9.
EL-OLAM: "*Everlasting God*" (God Of Everlasting Time) Gen. 21:33; Psa. 90:1-3, 93:2; Isa. 26:4.
EL-GIBHOR: Mighty God, God The Warrior (Isaiah 9:6)
ZUR: "*God Our Rock*" Deut. 32:18; Isa. 30:29.
'Attiq Yomin (Aramaic): "*Ancient Of Days,*" Dan. 7:9, 13, 22.
MELEKH:"*King*" Psa. 5:2, 29:10, 44:4, 47:6-8, 48:2, 68:24, 74:12, 95:3, 97:1, 99:4, 146:10; Isa. 5:1, 5, 41:21, 43:15, 44:6; 52:7, 52:10.
FATHER: 2 Sam. 7:14-15; Psa. 68:5; Isa. 63:16, 64:8; Mal. 1:6.
THE FIRST AND LAST: Isa. 44:6, 48:12.

2. The Names of Jesus- My Elder Brother I reverence
   You are my Advocate (1 John 2:1)
   You are my Almighty (Rev. 1:8; Mt. 28:18)
   You are my Atoning Sacrifice for our Sins (1 John 2:2)
   You are my Author of Life (Acts 3:15)
   You are my Author and Perfecter of our Faith (Heb. 12:2)
   You are my Author of Salvation (Heb. 2:10)
   You are my Beginning and End (Rev. 22:13)
   You are my Bread of Life (John 6:35; 6:48)
   You are my Bridegroom (Mt. 9:15)
   You are my Chief Shepherd (1 Pet. 5:4)
   You are my Christ (1 John 2:22)
   You are my Creator (John 1:3)
   You are my Deliverer (Rom. 11:26)
   You are my Eternal Life (1 John 1:2; 5:20)
   You are my Gate (John 10:9)
   You are my Faithful and True Witness (Rev. 3:14)
   You are my Firstborn From the Dead (Rev. 1:5)
   You are my Firstborn over all creation (Col. 1:15)
   You are my Gate (John 10:9)
   You are my God (John 1:1; 20:28; Heb. 1:8; Rom. 9:5; 2 Pet. 1:1;1 John 5:20; etc.)

You are my Great Shepherd (Heb. 13:20)
You are my Great High Priest (Heb. 4:14)
You are my Head of the Church (Eph. 1:22; 4:15; 5:23)
You are my Heir of all things (Heb. 1:2)
You are my Holy One (Acts 3:14)
You are my Hope of Glory (Col. 1:27)
You are my Image of God (2 Cor. 4:4)
You are my Judge of the living and the dead (Acts 10:42)
You are my King of kings (1 Tim 6:15; Rev. 19:16)
You are my Lamb Without Blemish (1 Pet. 1:19)
You are my Life (John 14:6; Col. 3:4)
You are my Light of the World (John 8:12)
You are my Lord of All (Acts 10:36)
You are my Lord of Glory (1 Cor. 2:8)
You are my Mighty God (Isa. 9:6)
You are the Offspring of David (Rev. 22:16)
You are the Only Begotten Son of God (John 1:18; 1 John 4:9)
You are my Great God and Savior (Titus 2:13)
You are my Holiness (1 Cor. 1:30)
You are my Husband (2 Cor. 11:2)
You are my Protection (2 Thess. 3:3)
You are my Redemption (1 Cor. 1:30)
You are my Righteousness (1 Cor. 1:30)
You are my Sacrificed Passover Lamb (1 Cor. 5:7)
You are my Power of God (1 Cor. 1:24)
You are my Prophet (Acts 3:22)
You are my Resurrection and Life (John 11:25)
You are my Rock (1 Cor. 10:4)
You are my Ruler of God's Creation (Rev. 3:14)
You are my Ruler of the Kings of the Earth (Rev. 1:5)
You are my Savior (Eph. 5:23; Titus 1:4; 3:6; 2 Pet. 2:20)
You are my Source of Eternal Salvation for all who obey him (Heb. 5:9)
You are my True Bread (John 6:32)
You are my True Light (John 1:9)
You are my Truth (John 1:14; 14:6)

You are my Way (John 14:6)
You are my Wisdom of God (1 Cor. 1:24)
You are my Word of God (Rev. 19:13)

3. According to your word: Confessions

Hebrews 1:3: *The Son is the radiance of God's glory and the exact representation of his being, sustaining all things by his powerful word. After he had provided purification for sins, he sat down at the right hand of the Majesty in heaven.*

I am a glory carrier because he lives in me.

Romans 8:17: *Now if we are children, then we are heirs—heirs of God and co-heirs with Christ, if indeed we share in his sufferings in order that we may also share in his glory.*

I am a co-heir with Christ

Philippians 4:13: *I can do everything through him who gives me strength.*

Christ in me the hope of Glory.

Philippians 4:19: *And my God will meet all my needs according to his glorious riches in Christ Jesus.*

1 John 4:4: *I am from God and have overcome the world, because the one who is in me is greater than the one who is in the world.*

1 John 5:4: *for everyone born of God overcomes the world. This is the victory that has overcome the world, even our faith.*

Romans 8:25-35:
[25] *But if we hope for what we do not yet have, we wait for it patiently.* [26] *In the same way, the Spirit helps us in our weakness. We do not know what we ought to pray for, but the Spirit himself intercedes for us with groans that words cannot express.* [27] *And he who searches our hearts knows the mind of the Spirit, because the Spirit intercedes for the saints in accordance with God's will.* [28] *And we know that in all things God works for the good of those*

who love him, who have been called according to his purpose. ²⁹For those God foreknew he also predestined to be conformed to the likeness of his Son, that he might be the firstborn among many brothers. ³⁰And those he predestined, he also called; those he called, he also justified; those he justified, he also glorified. ³¹What, then, shall we say in response to this? If God is for us, who can be against us? ³²He who did not spare his own Son, but gave him up for us all—how will he not also, along with him, graciously give us all things? ³³Who will bring any charge against those whom God has chosen? It is God who justifies. ³⁴Who is he that condemns? Christ Jesus, who died—more than that, who was raised to life—is at the right hand of God and is also interceding for us. ³⁵Who shall separate us from the love of Christ? Shall trouble or hardship or persecution or famine or nakedness or danger or sword?

    4. Pray in the Spirit: Intercessor; to encourage yourself, to liven up your faith.

Romans 8:26-28: *²⁶In the same way, the Spirit helps us in our weakness. We do not know what we ought to pray for, but the Spirit himself intercedes for us with groans that words cannot express. ²⁷And he who searches our hearts knows the mind of the Spirit, because the Spirit intercedes for the saints in accordance with God's will. ²⁸And we know that in all things God works for the good of those who love him, who have been called according to his purpose.*

I Corinthians 14:2, 4-5: *²For anyone who speaks in a tongue does not speak to men but to God. Indeed, no one understands him; he utters mysteries with his spirit. ⁴He who speaks in a tongue edifies himself, but he who prophesies edifies the church. ⁵I would like every one of you to speak in tongues, but I would rather have you prophesy. He who prophesies is greater than one who speaks in tongues, unless he interprets, so that the church may be edified.*

Jude 17-21: *¹⁷But, dear friends, remember what the apostles of our Lord Jesus Christ foretold. ¹⁸They said to you, "In the last times there will be scoffers who will follow their own ungodly desires."*

[19] *These are the men who divide you, who follow mere natural instincts and do not have the Spirit.* [20] *But you, dear friends, build yourselves up in your most holy faith and pray in the Holy Spirit.* [21] *Keep yourselves in God's love as you wait for the mercy of our Lord Jesus Christ to bring you to eternal life.*

The Ark of the Covenant- The Place of Intimacy and Intercession

Now Father, I come to the place of ultimate joy. Your Word says:

Psalm 16:11, [11] *You have made known to me the path of life; you will fill me with joy in your presence, with eternal pleasures at your right hand.*

Neh 8:10, [10] *Nehemiah said, "Go and enjoy choice food and sweet drinks, and send some to those who have nothing prepared. This day is sacred to our Lord. Do not grieve, for the joy of the LORD is your strength."*

John 17: 20-23, [20] *"My prayer is not for them alone. I pray also for those who will believe in me through their message,* [21] *that all of them may be one, Father, just as you are in me and I am in you. May they also be in us so that the world may believe that you have sent me.* [22] *I have given them the glory that you gave me, that they may be one as we are one:* [23] *I in them and you in me. May they be brought to complete unity to let the world know that you sent me and have loved them even as you have loved me.*

Acts 12:5, [5] *So Peter was kept in prison, but the church was earnestly praying to God for him.*

I therefore prepare my heart to love on you more and intercede for others.

A. I love you, I love you, I love you, I worship you, I adore you... No one like you...

B. ***Psalm 16:11:*** *You have made known to me the path of life; you will fill me with joy in your presence, with eternal pleasures at your right hand.*

C. *Intercession According to your Word:*

    1. ***John 17:20-23:*** *20"My prayer is not for them alone. I pray also for those who will believe in me through their message, [21]that all of them may be one, Father, just as you are in me and I am in you. May they also be in us so that the world may believe that you have sent me. [22]I have given them the glory that you gave me that they may be one as we are one: [23]I in them and you in me. May they be brought to complete unity to let the world know that you sent me and have loved them even as you have loved me.*

    2. ***Acts 12:5:*** *So Peter was kept in prison, but the church was earnestly praying to God for him.*

    3. I enter with faith and confidence into the Holy of Holies. I see the blood of Jesus Christ sprinkled on the Mercy seat. It is finished. All my debts have been paid off – paid in full. I am a free man, free from bondage to sin of any kind. Through the Blood I have the impartation of the righteousness of Jesus Christ! I am God's righteousness in Christ. I come into the presence of God without feeling any condemnation because of what Christ has already accomplished for me. The blood is the answer – it is the final solution for me. I praise you, Father, for the wonderful, incredible blessing of righteousness imparted to me, your servant, through your Son, Jesus Christ. I pray for those closest to me and work out from there like a stone making a ripple on the water. Now I am

truly ready to have my prayers answered and my petitions heard. I bring them humbly before you Lord with faith and confidence that you hear me and will answer my prayers.

    a. I have made my heart your residence- I am the Ark of the new covenant
    b. Covenant Compassion- loving on him and living with and in him.

    c. Thank you that our relationship and our fellowship, gives me a right to come before you boldly with requests.

    d. ***John 16:23:*** *In that day you will no longer ask me anything. I tell you the truth, my Father will give you whatever you ask in my name.*

4. A prayer list of people
   a. People in authority
      i. Governments
         World Leaders- President, Congress and Senators
      ii. Church- Bishops, Pastors, Apostles, Teachers, Prophets, Evangelists, Worship leaders, Missionaries, Elders, Helps Ministries, Support Staff, Music & Arts
      iii. Job- boss, coworkers
      iv. Home- spouse, children, parents, siblings
      v. Law enforcement
      vi. Business Owners
   b. Enemies
   c. Friends
   d. Extended Family
   e. Health Challenged
   f. Lost
   g. Youth

5. I pray for leaders in the church who are in bondage- Matt 9: 36-38

Matthew 9:36-38: *³⁶When he saw the crowds, he had compassion on them, because they were harassed and helpless, like sheep without a shepherd. ³⁷Then he said to his disciples, "The harvest is plentiful but the workers are few. ³⁸Ask the Lord of the harvest, therefore, to send out workers into his harvest field."*

Chapter 10 "A Call to Intercession"

"Oh, that one might plead for a man with God, as a man pleadeth for his neighbor!" Job 16:21 (KJV)

Intercession means, pray or petition in favor of another. I do believe that everyone must be a mediator or intercessor. As believers, we are called to pray for our families, leaders, people in authority and Israel. God has chosen those of us who believe to stand in the gap and transform the world. In Ezekiel 22:30-31, God is searching for anyone who can act as the person to close the gap between Him and men, but found none. There was no one who was giving up their own will and turning their hearts over to Him. A ministry of intercession requires a person who has fully and whole-heartedly given himself or herself over to Christ, submitting completely to the Holy Spirit to guide them. An intercessor gives all praise and glory to God. They must keep a clean and open heart to hear God's direction, and they must possess enough strength to stand against the enemy. *"...The earnest prayer of a righteous person has great power and wonderful results" (James 5:16).* While we all must be an intercessor as Christians, we are all not burdened with the desire to intercede for others. A calling therefore is needed. I must pray for people, cities and churches. If you feel that God has indeed called you as an intercessor, the place where intercession must start is with you. It's great to know that other people may be stepping up and spending time in prayer for someone before God, but as an intercessor, God wants you to put something of yourself on the line. If God's love is truly at work in you, you will care about others, and your love for them will lead you to take it to the Father, the ultimate Source of strength, healing, and love. Don't be fearful; be persistent and stubborn. God doesn't mind; God likes to see divine love at work in you. God honors your part in the relationship. Always remember that you are never praying alone. When the love in you for other people causes you to ask God to act; to strengthen, heal, defend, change, or bless them, there is someone else praying with you: the Holy Spirit. Intercessory prayer is prayed in a 'Trinitarian' manner: to the Father, through the Son, and in and with the Holy Spirit. So you are never alone. Even in times when your mind is not clear, the Spirit steps in for you, to convey the prayer and then draw you into it. Anyone can pray for others and step in with God on their behalf. But some people are gifted at intercession. They have an ear for the needs of others, and take them before God even when those other people reject God. If that sounds like you, then you may be a gifted intercessor.

What Is Intercessory Prayer?

Intercessory prayer is not praying on your own behalf for spiritual gifts, or for guidance, or any personal matter, or any material blessings. Simply stated, intercessory prayer is the act of praying on the behalf of others. However, we must understand that intercessory prayer actually goes beyond a simple prayer for others. An intercessor is one who takes the place of another or pleads another's case. An intercessor is actually acting as a mediator between God and the person or people he or she is praying for. An intercessor stands in and closes the gap. A prayer of intercession is fervent, holy, believing, and persevering. It is prayed with the full expectation that God will act. A Biblical Foundation The background for the call to intercession is found in the Old Testament example of the Levitical priesthood. The priest's responsibility was to stand before and between. He stood before God to minister to Him with sacrifices and offerings. The priests also stood between a righteous God and sinful man bringing them together at the place of the blood sacrifice. The New Testament basis for the believer's ministry of intercessory prayer is our calling as priests unto God. The Word of God declares that we are a holy priesthood (*1 Peter 2:5- you also, like living stones, are being built into a spiritual house to be a holy priesthood, offering spiritual sacrifices acceptable to God through Jesus Christ.*), a royal priesthood (*1 Peter 2:9: But you are a chosen people, a royal priesthood, a holy nation, a people belonging to God, that you may declare the praises of him who called you out of darkness into his wonderful light.*), and a kingdom of priests (*Revelation 1:5: Grace and peace to you from him who is, and who was, and who is to come, and from the seven spirits before his throne, ⁵and from Jesus Christ, who is the faithful witness, the firstborn from the dead, and the ruler of the kings of the earth.*). Hebrews 7:11-19 explains the difference between the Old and New Testament ministries of the priest. The Old Testament Levitical priesthood was passed on from generation to generation through the descendants of the tribe of Levi. The Melchizedek priesthood spoken of in this passage is the new order of spiritual priests of whom the Lord Jesus is the High Priest. It is passed on to us through His blood and our spiritual birth as new creatures in Christ. Our Model Intercessor Jesus Christ is our model for intercessory prayer. Jesus stands before God and between Him and sinful man, just as the Old Testament priests did: For there is one God, and one mediator (intercessor) between God and men, the man Christ Jesus (*1 Timothy 2:5: For there is one God and one mediator between God and men, the man Christ Jesus*). It is Christ who died, and furthermore is also risen, who is even at the right hand of God, who also makes intercession for us (*Romans 8:34: Who is he that condemns? Christ Jesus, who died—more than that, who was raised to life—is at the right hand of God and is also interceding for us.*). Therefore He is also able to save to the uttermost those who come to God through Him, since He always lives to make intercession for them (*Hebrews 7:25: Therefore he is able to save completely those who come to God through him, because he always lives to intercede for them.*).

    The sin of man brought a gap between God and man. Then Jesus was born and closed the gap between God and us when He died on the cross. He was the greatest mediator (intercessor) that ever lived. *He prayed for those* who were sick and possessed by demons. He prayed for His disciples. He even prayed for you and me when He interceded for all those who would believe on Him. Jesus brings sinful man and a righteous God together at the place of the blood sacrifice for sin. No longer is the blood of animals necessary as it was in the Old Testament. We can now approach God on the basis of the blood of Jesus that was shed on

the cross of Calvary for the remission of sins. Because of the blood of Jesus, we can approach God boldly without timidity
Hebrews 4:14-16: ⁴Therefore, since we have a great high priest who has gone through the heavens, Jesus the Son of God, let us hold firmly to the faith we profess. ¹⁵For we do not have a high priest who is unable to sympathize with our weaknesses, but we have one who has been tempted in every way, just as we are—yet was without sin. ¹⁶Let us then approach the throne of grace with confidence, so that we may receive mercy and find grace to help us in our time of need.

Because of this we can now intercede in prayer on behalf of other Christians, or for the lost, causing them to repent and seek after God. "For there is one God and one Mediator between God and men, the Man Christ Jesus" (1 Timothy 2:5). Jesus continued His ministry of intercession after His death and resurrection when He returned to Heaven. He now serves as our intercessor in Heaven. "Who is he who condemns? It is Christ who died, and furthermore is also risen, who is even at the right hand of God, who also makes intercession for us" (Romans 8:34). Effective Intercession In intercessory prayer, we follow the Old Testament priestly function and the New Testament pattern of Jesus - standing before God and between a righteous God and sinful man. In order to be effective standing "between" we must first stand "before" God to develop the intimacy necessary to fulfill this role. Numbers 14 is one of the greatest accounts of intercessory prayer recorded in the Bible. Moses was able to stand between God and sinful man because he had stood "before" Him and had developed intimacy of communication. Numbers 12:8 records that God spoke with Moses as friend to friend and not through visions and dreams as He did with other prophets.

As New Testament believers we stand before the Lord to offer up sacrifices of praise (*Hebrews 13:15: ¹⁵Through Jesus, therefore, let us continually offer to God a sacrifice of praise—the fruit of lips that confess his name.*) and the sacrifice of our own lives (*Romans 12:1 Therefore, I urge you, brothers, in view of God's mercy, to offer your bodies as living sacrifices, holy and pleasing to God—this is your spiritual act of worship.*). It is on the basis of this intimate relationship with God that we can then stand "between" Him and others, serving as an advocate and intercessor in their behalf. Peter uses two words to describe this priestly ministry: "Holy" and "royal." Holiness is required to stand before the Lord (Hebrews 12:14). We are able to do this only on the basis of the righteousness of Christ, not our own righteousness. Royalty is descriptive of the kingly authority that is delegated to us as members of the "royal family," so to speak, with legitimate access to the throne room of God.

Biblical Intercessors

Abraham's Prayer for Sodom

Genesis 18:20-33

20 Then the LORD said, "The outcry against Sodom and Gomorrah is so great and their sin so grievous 21 that I will go down and see if what they have done is as bad as the outcry that has reached me. If not, I will know." 22 The men turned away and went toward Sodom, but Abraham remained standing before the LORD. 23 Then Abraham approached him and said: "Will you sweep away the righteous with the wicked? 24 What if there are fifty righteous people in the city? Will you really sweep it away and not spare the place for the sake of the fifty righteous people in it? 25 Far be it from you to do such a thing—to kill the righteous with the wicked, treating the righteous and the wicked alike. Far be it from you! Will not the Judge of all the earth do right?" 26 The LORD said, "If I find fifty righteous people in the city of Sodom, I will spare the whole place for their sake." 27 Then Abraham spoke up again: "Now that I have been so bold as to speak to the Lord, though I am nothing but dust and ashes, 28 what if the number of the righteous is five less than fifty? Will you destroy the whole city because of five people?" "If I find forty-five there," he said, "I will not destroy it." 29 Once again he spoke to him, "What if only forty are found there?" He said, "For the sake of forty, I will not do it." 30 Then he said, "May the Lord not be angry, but let me speak. What if only thirty can be found there?" He answered, "I will not do it if I find thirty there." 31 Abraham said, "Now that I have been so bold as to speak to the Lord, what if only twenty can be found there?" He said, "For the sake of twenty, I will not destroy it." 32 Then he said, "May the Lord not be angry, but let me speak just once more. What if only ten can be found there?" He answered, "For the sake

of ten, I will not destroy it." ₃₃ *When the LORD had finished speaking with Abraham, he left, and Abraham returned home.*

Moses Prayer, Interceding For Israel

Exodus 32:11-13

11 But Moses sought the favour of the LORD his God. "O LORD," he said, "why should your anger burn against your people, whom you brought out of Egypt with great power and a mighty hand? 12 Why should the Egyptians say, 'It was with evil intent that he brought them out, to kill them in the mountains and to wipe them off the face of the earth'? Turn from your fierce anger; relent and do not bring disaster on your people. 13 Remember your servants Abraham, Isaac and Israel, to whom you swore by your own self: 'I will make your descendants as numerous as the stars in the sky and I will give your descendants all this land I promised them, and it will be their inheritance forever.' "

Exodus 32:31-32

31 So Moses went back to the LORD and said, "Oh, what a great sin these people have committed! They have made themselves gods of gold. 32 But now, please forgive their sin-but if not, then blot me out of the book you have written."

Ezra's Prayer

Ezra 9:6-15

"O my God, I am too ashamed and disgraced to lift up my face to you, my God, because our sins are higher than our heads and our guilt has reached to the heavens. 7 From the days of our forefathers until now, our guilt has been great. Because of our sins, we and our kings and our priests have been subjected to the sword and captivity, to pillage and humiliation at the hand of foreign kings, as it is today. 8 "But now, for a brief moment, the LORD our God has been gracious in leaving us a remnant and giving us a firm place in his sanctuary, and so our God gives light

to our eyes and a little relief in our bondage. 9 Though we are slaves, our God has not deserted us in our bondage. He has shown us kindness in the sight of the kings of Persia: He has granted us new life to rebuild the house of our God and repair its ruins, and he has given us a wall of protection in Judah and Jerusalem. 10 "But now, O our God, what can we say after this? For we have disregarded the commands 11 you gave through your servants the prophets when you said: 'The land you are entering to possess is a land polluted by the corruption of its peoples. By their detestable practices they have filled it with their impurity from one end to the other. 12 Therefore, do not give your daughters in marriage to their sons or take their daughters for your sons. Do not seek a treaty of friendship with them at any time, that you may be strong and eat the good things of the land and leave it to your children as an everlasting inheritance.' 13 "What has happened to us is a result of our evil deeds and our great guilt, and yet, our God, you have punished us less than our sins have deserved and have given us a remnant like this. 14 Shall we again break your commands and intermarry with the peoples who commit such detestable practices? Would you not be angry enough with us to destroy us, leaving us no remnant or survivor? 15 O LORD, God of Israel, you are righteous! We are left this day as a remnant. Here we are before you in our guilt, though because of it not one of us can stand in your presence."

Elijah's Prayer

I Kings 18:36-37

At the time of sacrifice, the prophet Elijah stepped forward and prayed: "O LORD, God of Abraham, Isaac and Israel, let it be known today that you are God in Israel and that I am your servant and have done all these things at your command. Answer me, O LORD; answer me, so these people will know that you, O LORD, are God, and that you are turning their hearts back again."

Daniel's Prayer

Daniel 9:4-19

4 I prayed to the LORD my God and confessed:

"O Lord, the great and awesome God, who keeps his covenant of love with all who love him and obey his commands, 5 we have sinned and done wrong. We have been wicked and have rebelled; we have turned away from your commands and laws. 6 We have not listened to your servants the prophets, who spoke in your name to our kings, our princes and our fathers, and to all the people of the land. 7 "Lord, you are righteous, but this day we are covered with shame-the men of Judah and people of Jerusalem and all Israel, both near and far, in all the countries where you have scattered us because of our unfaithfulness to you. 8 O LORD, we and our kings, our princes and our fathers are covered with shame because we have sinned against you. 9 The Lord our God is merciful and forgiving, even though we have rebelled against him; 10 we have not obeyed the LORD our God or kept the laws he gave us through his servants the prophets. 11 All Israel has transgressed your law and turned away, refusing to obey you. "Therefore the curses and sworn judgments written in the Law of Moses, the servant of God, have been poured out on us, because we have sinned against you. 12 You have fulfilled the words spoken against us and against our rulers by bringing upon us great disaster. Under the whole heaven nothing has ever been done like what has been done to Jerusalem. 13 Just as it is written in the Law of Moses, all this disaster has come upon us, yet we have not sought the favour of the LORD our God by turning from our sins and giving attention to your truth. 14 The LORD did not hesitate to bring the disaster upon us, for the LORD our God is righteous in everything he does; yet we have not obeyed him. 15 "Now, O Lord our God, who brought your people out of Egypt with a mighty hand and who made for yourself a name that endures to this day, we have sinned, we have done wrong. 16 O Lord, in keeping with all your righteous acts, turn away your anger and your wrath from Jerusalem, your city, your holy hill. Our sins and the iniquities of our fathers have made Jerusalem and your people an object of scorn to all those around us. 17 "Now, our God, hear the prayer of your servant. For your sake, O Lord, look with favour on your desolate sanctuary. 18 Give ear, O God, and hear; open your eyes and see the desolation of the city that bears your Name. We do not make requests of you because we are righteous, but because of your great mercy. 19 O Lord, listen! O Lord, forgive! O Lord, hear

and act! For your sake, O my God, do not delay, because your city and your people bear your Name."

Nehemiah's Prayer

Nehemiah 1:3-11

3 They said to me, "Those who survived the exile and are back in the province are in great trouble and disgrace. The wall of Jerusalem is broken down, and its gates have been burned with fire." 4 When I heard these things, I sat down and wept. For some days I mourned and fasted and prayed before the God of heaven. 5 Then I said: "O LORD, God of heaven, the great and awesome God, who keeps his covenant of love with those who love him and obey his commands, 6 let your ear be attentive and your eyes open to hear the prayer your servant is praying before you day and night for your servants, the people of Israel. I confess the sins we Israelites, including myself and my father's house, have committed against you. 7 We have acted very wickedly toward you. We have not obeyed the commands, decrees and laws you gave your servant Moses. 8 "Remember the instruction you gave your servant Moses, saying, 'If you are unfaithful, I will scatter you among the nations, 9 but if you return to me and obey my commands, then even if your exiled people are at the farthest horizon, I will gather them from there and bring them to the place I have chosen as a dwelling for my Name.' 10 "They are your servants and your people, whom you redeemed by your great strength and your mighty hand. 11 O Lord, let your ear be attentive to the prayer of this your servant and to the prayer of your servants who delight in revering your name. Give your servant success today by granting him favour in the presence of this man."

And Nehemiah 9 (the whole chapter)

Jesus Intercedes for His Followers

John 17:6-26

6"I have revealed you to those whom you gave me out of the world. They were yours; you gave them to me and they have obeyed your word. 7Now they know that everything you have given me comes from you. ⁸For I gave them the words you gave me and they accepted them. They knew with certainty that I came from you, and they believed that you sent me. ⁹I pray for them. I am not praying for the world, but for those you have given me, for they are yours. ¹⁰All I have is yours and all you have is mine. And glory has come to me through them. ¹¹I will remain in the world no longer, but they are still in the world, and I am coming to you. Holy Father, protect them by the power of your name—the name you gave me— so that they may be one as we are one. ¹²While I was with them, I protected them and kept them safe by that name you gave me. None has been lost except the one doomed to destruction so that Scripture would be fulfilled. ¹³"I am coming to you now, but I say these things while I am still in the world, so that they may have the full measure of my joy within them. ¹⁴I have given them your word and the world has hated them, for they are not of the world any more than I am of the world. ¹⁵My prayer is not that you take them out of the world but that you protect them from the evil one. ¹⁶They are not of the world, even as I am not of it. ¹⁷Sanctify them by the truth; your word is truth. ¹⁸As you sent me into the world, I have sent them into the world. ¹⁹For them I sanctify myself, that they too may be truly sanctified.

"My prayer is not for them alone. I pray also for those who will believe in me through their message, that all of them may be one, Father, just as you are in me and I am in you. May they also be in us so that the world may believe that you have sent me. I have given them the glory that you gave me, that they may be one as we are one: I in them and you in me. May they be brought to complete unity to let the world know that you sent me and have loved them even as you have loved me. "Father, I want those you have given me to be with me where I am, and to see my glory, the glory you have given me because you loved me before the creation of the world."Righteous Father, though the world does not know you, I know you, and they know that you have sent me. I have made you known to them, and will continue to make you known in order that the love you have for me may be in them and that I myself may be in them."

Stephen's Prayer

Acts 7:60

Then he fell on his knees and cried out, "Lord, do not hold this sin against them." When he had said this, he fell asleep.

Paul's Prayer For The Ephesians

Ephesians 3:14-20

For this reason I kneel before the Father, from whom his whole family in heaven and on earth derives its name. I pray that out of his glorious riches he may strengthen you with power through his Spirit in your inner being, so that Christ may dwell in your hearts through faith. And I pray that you, being rooted and established in love, 1may have power, together with all the believers, to grasp how wide and long and high and deep is the love of Christ, and to know this love that surpasses knowledge--that you may be filled to the measure of all the fullness of God. Now to him who is able to do immeasurably more than all we ask or imagine, according to his power that is at work within us, to him be glory in the church and in Christ Jesus throughout all generations, for ever and ever! Amen.

Paul's Prayer For The Philippians

Philippians 1:9-11

And this is my prayer: that your love may abound more and more in knowledge and depth of insight, so that you may be able to discern what is best and may be pure and blameless until the day of Christ, 11filled with the fruit of righteousness that comes through Jesus Christ--to the glory and praise of God.

Paul's Prayer For The Colossians

Colossians 1:9-17

For this reason, since the day we heard about you, we have not stopped praying for you and asking God to fill you with the knowledge of his will through all spiritual wisdom and understanding. And we pray this in order that you may live a life worthy of the Lord and may please him in every way: bearing fruit in every good work, growing in the knowledge of God, being strengthened with all power according to his glorious might so that you may have great endurance and patience, and joyfully giving thanks to the Father, who has qualified you to share in the inheritance.... in the kingdom of light. For he has rescued us from the dominion of darkness and brought us into the kingdom of the Son he loves, in whom we have redemption, the forgiveness of sins. He is the image of the invisible God, the firstborn over all creation. For by him all things were created: things in heaven and on earth, visible and invisible, whether thrones or powers or rulers or authorities; all things were created by him and for him. He is before all things, and in him all things hold together.

My beloved, go and be Christ in the earth. The whole earth is groaning, waiting for you the sons and daughters of God to be revealed. This is our season. Lift Him high. Know this as you go, that I will be praying for you. You are the favored of God. Go walk in your anointing. I believe in you. God believed in you enough to give you His Son. Now go believe in yourself. You are the Altared Life.

REFERENCES

Copyright 2004 © The Tabernacle Place. www.the-tabernacle-place.com

Prayer in the Hebrew Bible: The Drama of Divine-Human Dialogue, Samuel E. Balentine, Copyright ©1983 Published by Oxford University Press New York, NY

Victory Over Darkness, Neil T. Anderson, Copyright ©1990 by Regal Books, Copyright ©2000 by Neil T. Anderson, Published by Regal Books, A Division of Gospel Light, Ventura, CA.

The Oxford Classical Dictionary, Simon Hornblower (Editor) and Anthony Spawforth (Editor), Copyright © 2003, Published by Oxford University Press New York, NY

Funk & Wagnalls Standard Dictionary of Folklore, Mythology, and Legend, Copyright © 1984, Published by Harpers San Francisco, San Francisco, CA

Rediscovering New Testament Prayer, John Koenig, Copyright © 2004, Published by Wipf & Stock Publishers, Eugene, OR

Webster's II New Riverside Dictionary – Revised Edition, Copyright © 1996, Published by Houghton Mifflin Company, Boston, MA

The Mustard Seed Book, growing faith in your own backyard, Mike Flynn, Copyright ©1995, Published by Chosen Books a Division of Baker Book House Company, Grand Rapids, MI

My Journey With God: Your Personal Revival Journal Between You and God, Wellington Boone, Copyright ©2002

APPENDIX A

Scriptures

Unless noted, the following scriptures are from the Amplified version of the Bible.

For Healing:

James 5:15: [15]*And the prayer [that is] of faith will save him who is sick, and the Lord will restore him; and if he has committed sins, he will be forgiven.*

Luke 13:10-17: [10]*Now Jesus was teaching in one of the synagogues on the Sabbath.* [11]*And there was a woman there who for eighteen years had had an infirmity caused by a spirit (a demon of sickness). She was bent completely forward and utterly unable to straighten herself up or to look upward.* [12]*And when Jesus saw her, He called [her to Him] and said to her, Woman, you are released from your infirmity!* [13]*Then He laid [His] hands on her, and instantly she was made straight, and she recognized and thanked and praised God.* [14]*But the leader of the synagogue, indignant because Jesus had healed on the Sabbath, said to the crowd, There are six days on which work ought to be done; so come on those days and be cured, and not on the Sabbath day.* [15]*But the Lord replied to him, saying, you play actors (hypocrites)! Does not each one of you on the Sabbath loose his ox or his donkey from the stall and lead it out to water it?* [16]*And ought not this woman, a daughter of Abraham, whom Satan has kept bound for eighteen years, be loosed from this bond on the Sabbath day?* [17]*Even as He said this, all His opponents were put to shame, and all the people were rejoicing over all the glorious things that were being done by Him.*

Luke 17:11-19: [11]*As He went on His way to Jerusalem, it occurred that [Jesus] was passing [along the border] between Samaria and Galilee.* [12]*And as He was going into one village, He was met by ten* lepers, who stood at a distance. ¹³And they raised up their voices and called, Jesus, Master, take pity and have mercy on us! ¹⁴And when He saw them, He said to them, Go [at once] and show yourselves to the priests. And as they went, they were cured and made clean. ¹⁵Then one of them, upon seeing that he was cured, turned back, recognizing and thanking and praising God with a loud voice; ¹⁶And he fell prostrate at Jesus' feet, thanking Him [over and over]. And he was a Samaritan. ¹⁷Then Jesus asked, Were not [all] ten cleansed? Where are the nine? ¹⁸Was there no one found to return and to recognize and give thanks and praise to God except this alien? ¹⁹And He said to him, Get up and go on your way. Your faith (your trust and confidence that spring from your belief in God) has restored you to health.

Acts 3:1-10: ¹NOW PETER and John were going up to the temple at the hour of prayer, the ninth hour (three o'clock in the afternoon), ²[When] a certain man crippled from his birth was being carried along, who was laid each day at that gate of the temple [which is] called Beautiful, so that he might beg for charitable gifts from those who entered the temple. ³So when he saw Peter and John about to go into the temple, he asked them to give him a gift. ⁴And Peter directed his gaze intently at him, and so did John, and said, Look at us! ⁵And [the man] paid attention to them, expecting that he was going to get something from them. ⁶But Peter said, Silver and gold (money) I do not have; but what I do have, that I give to you: in [the use of] the name of Jesus Christ of Nazareth, walk! ⁷Then he took hold of the man's right hand with a firm grip and raised him up. And at once his feet and ankle bones became strong and steady, ⁸And leaping forth he stood and began to walk, and he went into the temple with them, walking and leaping and praising God. ⁹And all the people saw him walking about and praising God, ¹⁰And they recognized him as the man who usually sat [begging] for alms at the Beautiful Gate of the temple; and they were filled with wonder and amazement (bewilderment, consternation) over what had occurred to him.

For Deliverance

Mark 2:1-12: ¹AND JESUS having returned to Capernaum, after some days it was rumored about that He was in the house [probably Peter's]. ²And so many people gathered together there that there was no longer room [for them], not even around the door; and He was discussing the Word. ³Then they came, bringing a paralytic to Him, who had been picked up and was being carried by four men. ⁴And when they could not get him to a place in front of Jesus because of the throng, they dug through the roof above Him; and when they had scooped out an opening, they let down the [thickly padded] quilt or mat upon which the paralyzed man lay. ⁵And when Jesus saw their faith [their confidence in God through Him], He said to the paralyzed man, Son, your sins are forgiven [you] and put away [that is, the penalty is remitted, the sense of guilt removed, and you are made upright and in right standing with God]. ⁶Now some of the scribes were sitting there, holding a dialogue with themselves as they questioned in their hearts, ⁷Why does this Man talk like this? He is blaspheming! Who can forgive sins [remove guilt, remit the penalty, and bestow righteousness instead] except God alone? ⁸And at once Jesus, becoming fully aware in His spirit that they thus debated within themselves, said to them, Why do you argue (debate, reason) about all this in your hearts? ⁹Which is easier: to say to the paralyzed man, Your sins are forgiven and put away, or to say, Rise, take up your sleeping pad or mat, and start walking about [and keep on walking]? ¹⁰But that you may know positively and beyond a doubt that the Son of Man has right and authority and power on earth to forgive sins-- He said to the paralyzed man, ¹¹I say to you, arise, pick up and carry your sleeping pad or mat, and be going on home. ¹²And he arose at once and picked up the sleeping pad or mat and went out before them all, so that they were all amazed and recognized and praised and thanked God, saying, We have never seen anything like this before!

Mark 5:1-10: ¹THEY CAME to the other side of the sea to the region of the Gerasenes. ²And as soon as He got out of the boat, there met Him out of the tombs a man [under the power] of an unclean spirit. ³This man continually lived among the tombs, and no one could subdue him any more, even with a chain; ⁴For he had been bound often with shackles for the feet and handcuffs, but the handcuffs of [light] chains he wrenched apart, and the shackles he rubbed and ground together and broke in pieces; and no one had strength enough to restrain or tame him. [5]Night and day among the tombs and on the mountains he was always shrieking and screaming and beating and bruising and cutting himself with stones. [6]And when from a distance he saw Jesus, he ran and fell on his knees before Him in homage, [7]And crying out with a loud voice, he said, What have You to do with me, Jesus, Son of the Most High God? [What is there in common between us?] I solemnly implore you by God, do not begin to torment me! [8]For Jesus was commanding, Come out of the man, you unclean spirit! [9]And He asked him, What is your name? He replied, My name is Legion, for we are many. [10]And he kept begging Him urgently not to send them [himself and the other demons] away out of that region. [11]Now a great herd of hogs was grazing there on the hillside. [12]And the demons begged Him, saying, Send us to the hogs, that we may go into them! [13]So He gave them permission. And the unclean spirits came out [of the man] and entered into the hogs; and the herd, numbering about 2,000, rushed headlong down the steep slope into the sea and were drowned in the sea. [14]The hog feeders ran away, and told [it] in the town and in the country. And [the people] came to see what it was that had taken place. [15]And they came to Jesus and looked intently and searchingly at the man who had been a demoniac, sitting there, clothed and in his right mind, [the same man] who had had the legion [of demons]; and they were seized with alarm and struck with fear. [16]And those who had seen it related in full what had happened to the man possessed by demons and to the hogs. [17]And they began to beg [Jesus] to leave their neighborhood. [18]And when He had stepped into the boat, the man who had been controlled by the unclean spirits kept begging Him that he might be with Him. [19]But Jesus refused to permit him, but said to him, Go home to your own [family and relatives and friends] and bring back word to them of how much the Lord has done for you, and [how He has] had sympathy for you and mercy on you. [20]And he departed and began to publicly proclaim in Decapolis [the region of the ten cities] how much Jesus had done for him, and all the people were astonished and marveled.

Mark 9:14-29: [14]And when they came to the [nine] disciples, they saw a great crowd around them and scribes questioning and disputing with them. [15]And immediately all the crowd, when they saw Jesus [returning from the holy mount, His face and person yet *glistening], they were greatly amazed and ran up to Him [and] greeted Him.* ¹⁶*And He asked them, About what are you questioning and discussing with them?* ¹⁷*And one of the throng replied to Him, Teacher, I brought my son to you, for he has a dumb spirit.* ¹⁸*And wherever it lays hold of him [so as to make him its own], it dashes him down and convulses him, and he foams [at the mouth] and grinds his teeth, and he [falls into a motionless stupor and] is wasting away. And I asked Your disciples to drive it out, and they were not able [to do it].* ¹⁹*And He answered them, O unbelieving generation [without any faith]! How long shall I [have to do] with you? How long am I to bear with you? Bring him to Me.* ²⁰*So they brought [the boy] to Him, and when the spirit saw Him, at once it completely convulsed the boy, and he fell to the ground and kept rolling about, foaming [at the mouth].* ²¹*And [Jesus] asked his father, How long has he had this? And he answered, From the time he was a little boy.* ²²*And it has often thrown him both into fire and into water, intending to kill him. But if You can do anything, do have pity on us and help us.* ²³*And Jesus said, [You say to Me], If You can do anything? [Why,] all things can be (are possible) to him who believes!* ²⁴*At once the father of the boy gave [an eager, piercing, inarticulate] cry with tears, and he said, Lord, I believe! [Constantly] help my weakness of faith!* ²⁵*But when Jesus noticed that a crowd [of people] came running together, He rebuked the unclean spirit, saying to it, You dumb and deaf spirit, I charge you to come out of him and never go into him again.* ²⁶*And after giving a [hoarse, clamoring, fear-stricken] shriek of anguish and convulsing him terribly, it came out; and the boy lay [pale and motionless] like a corpse, so that many of them said, He is dead.* ²⁷*But Jesus took [a strong grip of] his hand and began lifting him up, and he stood.* ²⁸*And when He had gone indoors, His disciples asked Him privately, Why could not we drive it out?* ²⁹*And He replied to them, This kind cannot be driven out by anything but prayer and fasting.*

For Supernatural Occurrences

II Kings 2:1-8: ¹*WHEN THE Lord was about to take Elijah up to heaven by a whirlwind, Elijah and Elisha were going from Gilgal.* ²*And Elijah said to Elisha, Tarry here, I pray you, for the Lord has* sent me to Bethel. But Elisha replied, As the Lord lives and as your soul lives, I will not leave you. So they went down to Bethel. ³The prophets' sons who were at Bethel came to Elisha and said, Do you know that the Lord will take your master away from you today? He said, Yes, I know it; hold your peace. ⁴Elijah said to him, Elisha, tarry here, I pray you, for the Lord has sent me to Jericho. But he said, As the Lord lives and as your soul lives, I will not leave you. So they came to Jericho. ⁵The sons of the prophets who were at Jericho came to Elisha and said, Do you know that the Lord will take your master away from you today? And he answered, Yes; I know it; hold your peace. ⁶Elijah said to him, Tarry here, I pray you, for the Lord has sent me to the Jordan. But he said, As the Lord lives and as your soul lives, I will not leave you. And the two of them went on. ⁷Fifty men of the sons of the prophets also went and stood [to watch] afar off; and the two of them stood by the Jordan. ⁸And Elijah took his mantle and rolled it up and struck the waters, and they divided this way and that, so that the two of them went over on dry ground.

James 5:17: ¹⁷Elijah was a human being with a nature such as we have [with feelings, affections, and a constitution like ours]; and he prayed earnestly for it not to rain, and no rain fell on the earth for three years and six months.

Joshua 10:8-14: ⁸And the Lord said to Joshua, Do not fear them, for I have given them into your hand; there shall not a man of them stand before you. ⁹So Joshua came upon them suddenly, having gone up from Gilgal all night. ¹⁰And the Lord caused [the enemies] to panic before Israel, who slew them with a great slaughter at Gibeon and chased them along the way that goes up to Beth-horon and smote them as far as Azekah and Makkedah. ¹¹As they fled before Israel, while they were descending [the pass] to Beth-horon, the Lord cast great stones from the heavens on them as far as Azekah, killing them. More died because of the hailstones than the Israelites slew with the sword. ¹²Then Joshua spoke to the Lord on the day when the Lord gave the Amorites over to the Israelites, and he said in the sight of Israel, Sun, be silent and stand still at Gibeon, and you, moon, in the Valley of Ajalon! ¹³And the sun stood still, and the moon stayed, until the nation took vengeance upon their enemies. Is not this written in the Book of Jasher? So the sun stood still in the midst of the heavens and did *not hasten to go down for about a whole day.* ¹⁴*There was no day like it before or since, when the Lord heeded the voice of a man. For the Lord fought for Israel.*

Mark 11:12-25: ¹²*On the day following, when they had come away from Bethany, He was hungry.* ¹³*And seeing in the distance a fig tree [covered] with leaves, He went to see if He could find any [fruit] on it [for in the fig tree the fruit appears at the same time as the leaves]. But when He came up to it, He found nothing but leaves, for the fig season had not yet come.* ¹⁴*And He said to it, No one ever again shall eat fruit from you. And His disciples were listening [to what He said].* ¹⁵*And they came to Jerusalem. And He went into the temple [area, the porches and courts] and began to drive out those who sold and bought in the temple area, and He overturned the [four-footed] tables of the money changers and the seats of those who dealt in doves;* ¹⁶*And He would not permit anyone to carry any household equipment through the temple enclosure [thus making the temple area a short-cut traffic lane].* ¹⁷*And He taught and said to them, Is it not written, My house shall be called a house of prayer for all the nations? But you have turned it into a den of robbers.* ¹⁸*And the chief priests and the scribes heard [of this] and kept seeking some way to destroy Him, for they feared Him, because the entire multitude was struck with astonishment at His teaching.* ¹⁹*And when evening came on, He and His disciples, as accustomed, went out of the city.* ²⁰*In the morning, when they were passing along, they noticed that the fig tree was withered [completely] away to its roots.* ²¹*And Peter remembered and said to Him, Master, look! The fig tree which You doomed has withered away!* ²²*And Jesus, replying, said to them, Have faith in God [constantly].* ²³*Truly I tell you, whoever says to this mountain, Be lifted up and thrown into the sea! and does not doubt at all in his heart but believes that what he says will take place, it will be done for him.* ²⁴*For this reason I am telling you, whatever you ask for in prayer, believe (trust and be confident) that it is granted to you, and you will [get it].* ²⁵*And whenever you stand praying, if you have anything against anyone, forgive him and let it drop (leave it, let it go), in order that your Father Who is in heaven may also forgive you your [own] failings and shortcomings and let them drop.*

The following scriptures are taken from the New International Version:

Proverbs 1:1-7: [1] The proverbs of Solomon son of David, king of Israel: [2] for attaining wisdom and discipline; for understanding words of insight; [3] for acquiring a disciplined and prudent life, doing what is right and just and fair; [4] for giving prudence to the simple, knowledge and discretion to the young- [5] let the wise listen and add to their learning, and let the discerning get guidance- [6] for understanding proverbs and parables, the sayings and riddles of the wise. [7] The fear of the LORD is the beginning of knowledge, but fools despise wisdom and discipline.

Proverbs 4:5-12: [5] Get wisdom, get understanding; do not forget my words or swerve from them. [6] Do not forsake wisdom, and she will protect you; love her, and she will watch over you. [7] Wisdom is supreme; therefore get wisdom. Though it cost all you have, get understanding. [8] Esteem her, and she will exalt you; embrace her, and she will honor you. [9] She will set a garland of grace on your head and present you with a crown of splendor." [10] Listen, my son, accept what I say, and the years of your life will be many. [11] I guide you in the way of wisdom and lead you along straight paths. [12] When you walk, your steps will not be hampered; when you run, you will not stumble.

APPENDIX B
Sin List

A
Abandonment
Abduction
Abhorrence of holy things
Abhorring judgment
Abomination
Abortion
Abusiveness
Accusation
Adulterous lust
Adultery
Afflicting others
Aggravation
Agitation
Aiding and abetting sin
Alcoholism
All unrighteousness
anger
Animosity
Anxiety
Apprehension
Argumentativeness
Arrogance
Assaults
Astrology
Atheism
Avariciousness

B
Baal worship
Backbiting
Backsliding
Bad attitude
Bad language
Bearing false witness
Big talk
Being a workaholic
Being too quick to speak
Believing the lies of the enemy
Belittling
Bereavement
Betraying Jesus
Bickering
Bigotry
Bitterness
Black magic
Blackmail
Blasphemy
Blasphemy of the Holy Spirit
Boastfulness
Boisterousness
Bowing down to gods or serving images
Bragging
Brainwashing
Breaking commandments of God
Breaking vows and covenants to God
Breaking covenants and vows with others
Bribery
Brutality
Burning incense to gods

C
Calamity
Carelessness
Cares & riches of this world
Carnality
Casting God away
Causing conflict
Causing disagreements
Causing distress
Causing division
Causing fear
Causing men to err
Causing offense
Causing poor to fail
Changing truth to lies
Chanting of charms
Cheating
Committing willful and/or intentional sin
Complaining
Complacency against God's will or destiny
Conceit
Concupiscence
Condemnation
Condemning the just
Confrontation
Confusion
Conjuration
Conspiring against God
Consulting wizards and psychics
Contempt
Contention
Controlling
Conniving
Compulsiveness
Contentiousness
Contesting and withstanding and resisting God
Corruption
Counterfeiting
Christian work
Covering sin
Coveting neighbors spouse brother, sister, house, land, automobile or anything that is our neighbors
Covetousness
Cravenness
Criticalness
Crookedness
Cruelty
Crystal using
Cursing God
Cursing syndicalism

D
Dealing treacherously
Deceit
Deception
Defamation
Defeatism
Defiantness
Defiling
Degrading
Dejection
Demon consciousness
Demon worship
Denying Jesus and His

143

resurrection
Dependencies
Depravity
Desecration of holy
  vessels
Desires of this world
Despair
Despising God, His
  Name and His Word
Despising spouse
Despising neighbors
Despising parents
Despitefulness
Despondency
Destruction of the
  innocent, saints and
  holy things
Deviousness
Disagreements
Disbelief
Discord
Discouragement
discrediting
Disdain
Disgust
Dishonesty
Disliking the love of
  good men
Disobedience
Disobedient to God
Disorderly
Disputing
Disregard of God's
  work
Disrespectfulness of
  God Disruptiveness
Dissension
Distantness
Distrust
Divining
Divining for water
  with rods
Divining for money
Division
Divorce
Domineeringness
Double-talking
Double-mindedness
Doubt
Dread
Driving men from true
  worship and
  inheritance
Drug abuse
Drunkenness

Duplicity
Drinking blood

E
Eating blood
Eating sin offerings
Eating unclean food
Effeminate behavior
Egoism
Enchantment
Enlarged imaginations
Entering into ungodly
  soul ties
Entering into
  unrighteous
  agreements
Envy
Envy produced by lust
Escaping
Evil hearts or
  imaginations
Exasperation
Extortion

F
Failure in duty
Failure to glorify God
False burdens
False compassion
Falsehood
False praise
False responsibility
Fantasizing
Fantasy lust
Fault finding
Fear
Fear of accusation
Fear of condemnation
Fear of disapproval
Fear of man
Fear of rejection
Fear of failure
Fear of reproof
Fetishes
Fighting
Flattery
Fleshliness
Fooling self and/or
  others Foolishness
Following any ways of
  man
Folly
Forbidding the
  preaching of God's
  Word
Forcefulness

Forgetting God and
  His work
Fornication
Forsaking the
  assembly
Fortune telling
Fraud
Fretting frigidity
Frustrations
Fury

G
Gendering strife
Giving judgment for
  reward
Giving offense
Giving others alcohol
Gloominess
Gluttony
Gossip
Greed
Grieving God and the
  Holy Spirit
Grumbling
Guilt

H
Hard-hearted
Harlotry
Harshness
Hating
Hating God
Hating God's Word
Haughtiness
Having other gods
  before HIM
Headiness
High-minded
Holding God's table in
  contempt
Homosexuality
Hopelessness
Horoscopes
Human sacrifice
Hypocrisy

I
Idleness
Idolatries of any kind
Ignorance
Ignoring God
Ignoring His miracles
Ill will
Imitating true worship
Inhumanity

Imaginations
Immorality
Impatience
Impenitence
Impetuousness
Implacability
Imprudence
Impurity of thoughts
Impurity
Inadequacy
Incest
Incitement
Indecision
Independence
Indifferences
Inflating
Inflexibility
Inhospitality
Injustice
Inquiring of idols
Insolence
Intemperance
Intentional sins
Intimidation
Intolerances
Intellectualism and
   sophistication
Inventing evil
Inventing sin
Inward wickedness
Irrationality
Irreverence

J-K
Jealousy
Judging others
Justifying the wicked
Kidnapping
Killing

L
Lack of self-control
Lawlessness
Laying in wait to sin
Lasciviousness
Laziness
Legalism
Lesbianism
Levitation
Lewdness
Limiting God
Lip service

Living contrary to
nature
Loathing
Longing for sin
Loneliness
Loose morals
Looting
Loving to curse
Loving evil
loving money
loving to be chief
loving human titles
Loving human praise
Lust
Lust of the eye
Lust of the flesh
Lust of the mind
Lying
Lying to the Holy
Spirit
Lying with pleasure
and delight

M
Madness
Magic
Male prostitution
Making or buying
images
Making false vows
Making God a liar
Making war
Maliciousness
Manipulation
Manslaughter
Marauding
Masturbation
Materialism
Meanness
Misbelieving
Mischief
Misery
Misleading
Misuse of the law
Mocking
Mulishness
Murder
Murmuring
Murmuring about
wages
Muttering

N
Necromancy
Negativism
Nervous habits
Nicotine addiction
Not having a
conscience
Not being a good
steward of Your
money
Not fearing God
Not giving to the poor
Not honoring fathers
and   mothers
Not letting go of
wickedness
Not loving God with
all our heart, soul and
mind
Not loving our
neighbor as our self
Not loving our self
Not observing and
keeping holy the
Sabbath day
Not praising and
worshiping God the
way we should and
when we should and
how we should
Not being watchful

O-P-Q
Obsessing
Obstinacy,
Occultism
Offering polluted
sacrifices
Opposing the gospel
Oppressing widows
and orphans
Oppression
Overbearing
Pastors destroying and
   scattering sheep
Pedophilia
Pendulum
Persecuting believers
Persecuting the poor
Persecution
Perversion
Perverting the gospel

145

Perverting truth for personal gain
Petulance
Planning without God
Plotting
Plundering
Polluting God's house and Sabbaths
Pompousness
Pornography
Possessiveness
Pouting
Prayerlessness
Prejudice
Presumption
Pretending to be a prophet
Pretension
Prideful
Pride of life
Procrastination
Profane God and His holiness
Profanity unto God
Professing to be wise
Prophecy by Baal
Prophesying lies
Propagating lies
Proudest
Provoking God
Provoking
Puffing up
Quarreling
Quenching the Holy Spirit
Questioning God's word

R
Raiding
Railing
Raging
Raping
Rationalization
Ravaging
Rebellion
Rebuking the Lord
Recklessness
Refusing correction
Refusing to hear
Refusing to repent
Refusing to destroy ungodly altars
Refusing to be humble
Refusing to live in peace
Regarding iniquity in your heart
Rejecting reproof
Rejecting salvation
Rejecting God and His Word
Rejection
Rejoicing in others' adversity
Rejoicing in idols
Rejoicing in iniquity
Repetitiveness
Reproaching good men
Requiring usury
Resentment
Restlessness
Retaliation
Returning evil for good
Returning hate for love
Reveling
Reviling
Revenge
Rewarding evil for good
Rigidity
Robbing God
Robbery
Rudeness

S
Sacrificing children to demons
Sadism
Scheming
Scornfulness
Scorning religion
Seduction
Seeking self gain
Seeking pleasures of this world
Seizing in an evil way
Self-accusations
Self-admiration
Self-centeredness
Self-condemnation
Self-corruption
Self-criticalness
Self-deception
Self-delusion
Self-destruction
Self-exultation
Self-glorification
Self-hatred
Self-importance
Self-rejection
Selfishness
Self-pity
Self-righteousness
Self-seeking
Self-will
Serving other gods
Setting aside Godly counsel
Setting heart to sin
Sewing discord
Sexual idolatry
Sexual immorality
Sexual impurity
Sexual lewdness
Sexual perversion; oral sex, sodomy
Shame
Shamelessness
Silliness
Sin consciousness
Sinful mirth
Sissyness
Skepticism
Slander
Slaughter
Slaying
Slothfulness
Snobbishness
Soothsaying
Sorcery
Sowing seeds of hatred
Speaking incantations
Speaking folly
Speculation
Spell-casting
Spiritual laziness
Spitefulness
Stealing
Stiff-necked
Strife
Striving over leadership
Struggling
Stubbornness stupidity
Suicidal thoughts
Suspicion
Swallowing up the needy
Swearing to false gods
Swearing

T
Taking advantage of others

Taking a bribe
Taking offense
Taking God's Name in vain
Taking rights away from the poor
Teaching false doctrines
Temper
Temptation
Tempting God
Theft
Threatening disaster
Timidity
Teaching and tolerating wickedness
Tolerating false prophets
Tolerating sin and its ways
Tolerating wicked men
Trafficking with demons
Trickery
Two-facedness
Trusting lies
Trusting our own beauty
Trusting in our own righteousness
Trusting wickedness
Tumults
Turning to folly
Turning aside the way of the meek
Turning your back on God
Turning from righteousness
Turning aside for money

U-V
Unbelief
Unbridled lust
Uncleanness
Uncompromising
Undermining
Unequally yoked to non-believers
Unfairness
Unfaithfulness in trust
Unfaithfulness
Unforgiveness
Unfriendliness
Ungratefulness
Unholy alliances
Unholy habits
Unions with menstrual women
Unmanly
Unmercifulness
Unreadiness
Unrepenting,
Unrighteousness of laws
Unrighteousness
Unruliness of tongues
Unsparing
Un-submissiveness,
Unthankfulness
Untruthfulness
(being) unwise
Unworthiness
Using tarot cards
Vain imaginations
Vain repetitions
Vanity
Vengeance
Viciousness
Vile affections
Vile speaking
Violence
Vulgarity

W-Z
Walking after our own devices
Walking for unprofitable things
Walking after our own thoughts
Walking after false gods
Walking with heathens
Walking with sinners
Water witching
White magic
Wickedness
Willful sin
Willful blindness to the truth
Winking with evil intent
Witchcraft
Withdrawal
Withholding a pledge
(being) without concern
(being) without natural affection
(being) without mercy
Working iniquity
Working for praise
Worldliness
Worrying
Worshipping possessions,
Worshipping our works
Worshipping the creation instead of the Creator
Worshipping of planets
Wrathfulness
Wrong doing
Zealousness to make others sinful
Zealousness in outward show.

ABOUT THE AUTHOR

Bishop Darryl F. Husband is the Senior Pastor of Mount Olivet Church and founder of Life More Abundant Ministries. Bishop Husband's philosophy "You Can Have What You Say," is a faith based ministry that crosses cultures to change lives. His heart is one of a father, helping pastors and churches reach their full potential. These changes will help God's people to exhibit habits of godliness in every area of their lives, leading to what is written in John 10:10 "I came that they may have life, and may have it more abundantly."

Bishop Husband has several spiritual connections. He is connected to Bishop Wellington Boone's Fellowship of International Churches, under whom he was laid hands upon and received the mantle of a bishop in the Lords church. He and Co-Pastor Sherrine C. Husband were ordained in the Word of Faith ministries by Drs. Ira and Bridgett Hilliard. He also serves the Full Gospel Church Fellowship International as the Southern-Atlantic Regional Director for the International Intercessory Prayer Ministry, where Bishop Paul S. Morton is the presiding Bishop.

For more than 25 years he has served as Senior Pastor to the Mount Olivet Church and now L.I.F.E Church, two locations one multi-cultural congregation. He truly believes that the Church should look like heaven, every nationality in worship to God.

Dr. Husband received his Bachelor's degree from Illinois State University in Foreign Language. He later matriculated at Virginia Union University where he earned his Master's degree in Divinity at the Samuel D. Proctor School of Theology. He later went on to earn a Doctor of Ministry degree in 2004 from Virginia University of Lynchburg. He has also done doctoral studies at Boston University.

He is married to the former Sherrine Charity, and they are the proud parents of, Jason Oliver, Darryl Frederick Husband II, Gabriella Sherrine Agape Husband, Daytriel McQuinn and Eric Elam.

The Altared Life is a testimony of his life and at the heart of his beliefs of how the church today will make the turn towards being truly examples of what it looks like to be made in the "image of God". We are the Word made flesh for the world to read and emulate. His favorite phrase at the end of worship is fitting as you conclude this reading, "You are the favored of God, go walk in your anointing".